T0330961

International Competitiveness in

Latin America and East Asia

INTERNATIONAL COMPETITIVENESS IN LATIN AMERICA AND EAST ASIA

KLAUS ESSER,
WOLFGANG HILLEBRAND,
DIRK MESSNER and
JÖRG MEYER-STAMER

FRANK CASS • LONDON
Published in association with the
German Development Institute, Berlin

First published in 1993 in Great Britain by
FRANK CASS & CO. LTD.
2 Park Square, Milton Park,
Abingdon, Oxon, OX14 4RN

and in the United States of America by
FRANK CASS
270 Madison Ave,
New York NY 10016

Transferred to Digital Printing 2006

Copyright © 1993 GDI/Frank Cass

British Library Cataloguing in Publication Data

Esser. Klaus
    International Competitiveness in Latin
    America and East Asia.
    – (GDI Book Series: Vol. 1)
I. Title   II. Series
388.09

ISBN 0-7146-4541-9

Library of Congress Cataloging-in-Publication Data

International competitiveness in Latin America and
    East Asia / Klaus Esser . . . [et al.]
        p.   cm.
    "Published in association with the German Development Institute.
    Berlin."
        Includes bibliographical references.
        ISBN 0-7146-4541-9
        1. Industry and state – Latin America. 2. Competition – Latin
    America. 3. Forest products industry – Chile. 4. Machinery industry –
    Brazil. 5. Technological innovations – Korea (South)
    I. Esser. Klaus. II. Deutsches Institut für Entwicklungspolitik.
    HD3616.L32I54   1993
    338.6'048'098 – dc20   93-10464 CIP

Contents

Shaping Industrial Competitiveness in Chile.
The Case of the Chilean Wood-processing Industry

Dirk Messner

Comprehensive Modernization on the Shop-Floor:
A Case Study on the Machinery Industry in Brazil

Jörg Meyer-Stamer

Technological Modernization Processes in Korean Small-
and Medium-Scale Industry - a New Success Story

Wolfgang Hillebrand

Introduction and Summary

Latin America is undergoing a process of profound economic and social change. The industrial import substitution that continued for several decades was quantitatively successful in terms of industrialization but - like inward-oriented industrialization in the socialist countries - failed to raise the economies of the region to international productivity levels. The attempt at catch-up industrialization outside the reference frame of the world market led to economic stagnation, social crises, serious environmental degradation and the obstruction of social development.

The reorientation of economic policy in Latin America is strengthening market forces and has world-market-oriented specialization as its goal. In their search for a new paradigm most countries in the region are currently guided by the concept of the "free market economy". Neoliberal economic policies are helping to destroy the old structures, but they do not provide sufficient regulation to create the conditions needed for efficient markets. The social and environmental challenges are, moreover, being underestimated. The challenge in the 90s will be to improve the competitiveness of the economies but also to prepare for more equitable and sustainable growth.

The following papers show that the development of competitive advantages is initially determined by the the new macro policy and by modernization at enterprise level. A lasting improvement of locational advantages, however, calls for the active shaping of structures between the macro and micro levels ("meso level"). The success of industrial specialization in Latin America will depend on the ability of national actors to establish strategies that enable concepts beyond the neoliberal "pure open-economy strategy" to be developed and implemented. As there is much to be learnt from the experience of the East Asian newly industrializing countries in this respect, one of the papers looks beyond the Latin American horizon at the Republic of Korea.

The four papers examine different dimensions of the radical shift to world market orientation:

Klaus Esser shows how much the excessive inward orientation from 1930-90 influenced capitalism in Latin America. Enterprises there differ fundamentally from those of the industrialized countries. The long period of protection and the wide range of support they enjoyed kept the pressure off them, and their development options were few because of limited domestic demand. They came to rely more and more on "association-based corporatism", whose main aim was a further expansion of government promotion. Economic policy was increasingly geared to the interests of the associations. Once the potential for industrial import substitution was exhausted, the private sector's interest in investment quickly waned. By assuming ever greater responsibility for growth, government increased external indebtedness. Industrial enterprises often replaced their capital with foreign loans on what appeared to be favourable terms. At the same time capital flight and, therefore, external debts continued to rise.

From the late 80s, a lengthy and complex process of transition from inward orientation to world-market-oriented specialization began. Almost every country adopted US-style neoliberalism, there being no alternative economic policy. In many countries the public sector was radically reformed and tailored to the new economic objectives. Given the social and world economic requirements, however, the free market economy cannot be regarded as a sustainable paradigm. As soon as government has become efficient enough, it must not only ensure a stable macro framework but also help to improve the conditions for the economy to compete in the domestic, regional and world markets. Nor, with political, social and environmental problems quickly coming to a head in Latin America, is there any alternative to progressing from the free market economy to a socially oriented and sustainable competitive economy. It alone can improve the quality of democracy, now largely non-participatory.

Dirk Messner analyses the process of outward orientation and deregulation in Chile, where it began earlier than in the other Latin American countries. Lessons can thus be learnt from this case for the majority of the region's economies, which did not abandon the excessively inward-oriented development model until the late 80s. The Chilean wood-processing industry is an export sector that is developing dynamically and has considerable industrialization potential. Its competitiveness until the mid-80s largely stemmed from resource-based cost advantages and low wages. Exports consisted predominantly of such natural-resource-intensive products as round and sawn timber and cellulose. The attempt to advance into segments where value added is higher marks the end of "extensive growth" and the beginning of a "second export phase", in which the aim is to increase productivity by introducing modern technologies and forms of work organization.

The article reconstructs the process of the emergence of industrial competitiveness, revealing its systemic nature. The success of efforts to modernize enterprises and the creation of competitive advantages very much depend on improving the quality of the industrial environment. The "top performers" prove to be the enterprises which not only pursue internal rationalization strategies but also systematically optimize forms of an inter-company division of labour and cooperate with other enterprises, sectoral institutions and technological service organizations in improving the supply conditions they have in common. Viable sectoral structures are only now beginning to evolve, however. If there is to be a lasting improvement in the innovation potential of enterprises, it will be essential for this process to be accelerated with purposeful technology, industrial and training policies in the timber-producing regions. This will require cooperation among government and private institutions, enterprises and trade unions. The chances of this happening are not bad. The transition to democracy has led to political stability, the principal actors accept the model of a competition-oriented economy and are showing themselves to be capable of compromise, and decentralization - the prerequisite for an effective locational policy on the spot - appears to be making headway. It is becoming clear that concentration solely on macropolicy variables cannot do justice to the complexity of the shift to world market orientation.

Jörg Meyer-Stamer examines the revision of corporate strategies against the background of the radical changes in Brazil. With the economy gradually opening up, domestic and foreign enterprises in Brazil today face the challenge of significantly increasing their efficiency and capacity for innovation. Experience in the industrialized countries indicates that this will require the combined application of new manufacturing technologies and new organizational and social concepts ("new production concepts"), entailing flat hierarchies, a reduced division of labour and more highly skilled workforce.

The case study on the Brazilian mechanical engineering industry considers how far the previously mentioned innovations can be introduced in Brazil, a newly industrializing country. It shows that new production concepts have so far been viewed with scepticism or even rejected by foreign firms, whereas some domestic enterprises are implementing them very success-

whereas some domestic enterprises are implementing them very success-fully. The latter show, firstly, that even in an environment where the pres-sure to compete and so to be innovative is slight there are firms making a systematic effort to increase their productivity. The decision-makers in these firms are working on the principle that in Brazil as elsewhere survivial in the medium term will depend on efforts to be innovative. It is this that moti-vates them to introduce technical, organizational and social innovations; macro-level reorientation towards competition, on the other hand, has so far had little impact on enterprises and does not determine the way they act. Secondly, new production concepts are being implemented even when the political and socio-cultural environment has a deterrent effect. For the moment at least, the patriarchal structures that dominate in Brazilian enter-prises are not impeding the introduction of participatory organization models.

In his case study on Korea Wolfgang Hillebrand considers the strategies adopted by modern small and medium-sized enterprises in the footwear, machine tool and personal computer industries in order to hold their own as their labour cost advantages dwindle and international competition becomes fiercer. The analysis reveals that the particularly successful enterprises adapt to international "best practice". It is particularly important to note that technological and organizational innovations form an integral part of broadly based competitive strategies. Unterlying these strategies is a more or less explicitly formulated medium-term corporate strategy notable for its distinct orientation towards the market and customers, which is made the starting point for comprehensive internal and inter-company rationalization processes.

The competitive strength of the successful enterprises continues to stem from their selective use of external potential. Of prime importance is their strategy of cooperating closely in the development of ther R&D potential with local firms and especially foreign enterprises and R&D centres. They also make use of a fairly dense network of private and public institutions to overcome constraints in the areas of R&D, management, technology trans-fer, information procurement, marketing and financing. All in all, it is clear that highly complex corpórate strategies and capable intermediary organiza-tions are needed if international standards of efficiency are to be attained.

The last three of these papers are based on empirical studies carried out in Brazil, Chile and the Republic of Korea in the spring of 1991.

Latin America - Industrialization without Vision

Klaus Esser

1 Industrialization during the Period of Inward Orientation (1920-90): What is Left?

Three factors characterized the period from the end of the First World War until 1990: the expansion of socialism in response to capitalism, conflicts among the capitalist industrialized countries, which encouraged this countermovement, and after 1948 coordination among the capitalist industrialized countries, which made dynamic organizational, technical and financial development possible.

With the Russian Revolution efforts to accelerate industrialization along state-socialist lines began. After the Second World War further attempts at socialist industrialization were made. Economic integration in the socialist area was hampered by central planning, already overextended at national level, by inward orientation and by nationalism.

Another branch of the countermovement opposed not capitalism as such but the southward expansion of the capitalist industrialized countries. The Depression, which reduced imports and exports for a time, prompted most Latin American countries to experiment with inward-oriented industrialization from 1930 onwards. After the Second World War many Asian and African countries, having gained their political independence, similarly turned to inward-oriented capitalism. As in Latin America, nationalism and the "mixed economy" soon led to state-capitalist interventionism, which was principally geared to well organized private and, increasingly, to state-bureaucratic interests.

Both reactions to the capitalism of the industrialized countries foundered throughout the world in the 80s or early 90s. The question that therefore arises is how far "industrialization" was possible during state-socialist or state-capitalist inward orientation. Industry in the USSR and, to a lesser degree, Brazil was, after all, developed with the usual intra-industry vertical and horizontal linkages. It is now becoming clear, however, that to a great extent - to precisely what extent it is not yet known - the tremendous social efforts made in Eastern Europe and Latin America to industrialize were in vain.

Quantitative expansion has confused not a few researchers as to the quality of industrialization. It is estimated that no more than 50 to 100 enterprises in the former USSR and 300 to 500 in Brazil are at present internationally competitive. The depreciation of much of the industrial apparatus also diminishes the relevance of economic theories and policies that were geared to "inward-oriented industrialization".

2   Industrial Import Substitution: Not a Realistic Industrialization Concept

For six decades (1930-1990) an economic policy that sought to substitute domestic for imported manufactures was pursued in Latin America. The following five fundamental assumptions, on which industrial import substitution in Latin America was based, proved incorrect and misleading:

1) The import substitution policy was overly related to the industrial sector. Like socialist economic policy in Eastern Europe, it neglected the agricultural and service sectors. In Latin America it was assumed that "industrialization" would eventually make these two sectors of the economy more dynamic, but it had little or no impact on them. Hardly any of the agricultural reforms of the 60s helped to increase production and demand. For many years little advantage was taken of the potential for intersectoral linkages. Even in countries with very extensive agricultural potential, such as Argentina, the dynamism of the agricultural machinery and food-processing industries remained low.

2) Industrial import substitution depended on domestic demand with specific features: of crucial importance was demand arising from the greatest concentration of property and income in a comparison of the world's major regions. As the principal criterion of productivity development was neglected, the politics affecting wage levels changed with the importance attached to domestic demand and the political orientation of the government in power: in the 40s and 50s nationalist-populist governments in particular

helped to increase demand for simple manufactures by pursuing a generous wage policy. Once the development of more complex sectors, particularly the automobile industry, began in the industrially more advanced countries, and specifically in Brazil, in the mid-50s, it was found necessary to increase demand for the products of these sectors among the wealthiest 20 to 40 per cent of the population and, at times, even among the skilled workers, while generally reducing labour costs and increasing wage differentiation. When, in the late 60s, nothing more was to be gained from industrial import substitution, the employers, quickly followed by the governments, began trying to achieve a substantial reduction in real wages and to curtail the demands from the middle classes for better distribution. This, however, led to a further restriction of the scope for inward growth.

3) It was widely believed that any country, including the medium-sized and even the small, could achieve industrial import substitution in all sectors. It was, however, overlooked that because of inward orientation, industrial dynamism was essentially determined by the scale of domestic demand. Furthermore, organizational and technical factors mean that firms operate economically only when their total annual output reaches a certain level, which differs from one sector and product to another. It is an indication of a surprising absence of industrial policy foresight that at one time Peru had sixteen vehicle assembly plants (the three surviving in 1987 produced a total of 5,124 units)[1] and that in 1960 Argentina had 21 such plants (of which four were left in 1990, and their survival is threatened by import liberalization).[2] Plants of this kind were profitable because the closed market enabled prices to be maintained at a far higher level than comparable prices in the industrialized countries. For a long time quality could be virtually ignored. It is becoming clear how far aspects of efficiency could be neglected in an inward-oriented economy.

4) The United Nations Economic Commission for Latin America (CEPAL) in particular took the view that favourable conditions for international industrial competition would come only with the "integration of industry" as part of overall industrial development, including the capital goods industry. The efficiency of the capital goods industry in Brazil or Argentina, however, was little different from that of the rest of the industrial sector. In fact, the inefficiency of the capital goods and even the primary industry was mirrored throughout the production chain: the closer the vertical linkages in the industrial sector, the more difficult it was for the manufacturers of end products to produce them efficiently.

5) Finally, it was assumed that industrial import substitution would lead to an early reduction in imports of manufactures. Despite import substitution, or precisely because of it, they continued to rise, however, the main reason being that each new generation of machinery used in the industrialized countries was gradually introduced. As the Latin American countries did not set technological development in motion by their own efforts, unlike the countries of East Asia, and as the far from infrequent efforts to expose the economy to the growing pressure of imports by reducing external protection failed, there continued to be little pressure to export, and the ability to export therefore remained undeveloped. The economy, soon blocked within national boundaries, could not have been stimulated even by a more efficient monetary and credit system. As money and credit completely lost their function as guides during the period of inward orientation, the business community and government increasingly resorted to foreign borrowing. With investment opportunities also on the wane, the way into an external economic trap had long been predetermined. The debt crisis that began in 1982 is only one facet of Latin America's comprehensive strategy and development crisis.

3   Underexposed and Blocked Enterprises: Capitalism without an Efficient Private Sector

For many years the instruments of economic policy were chiefly geared to furthering industrial import substitution. They included:

-   high import tariffs and numerous non-tariff barriers,
-   a policy of low interest rates and inflationary government guarantees as protection against inflation and exchange rate risks,
-   low direct taxes and numerous tax exemptions and
-   high subsidies, reductions in the cost to industry of public services, such as energy, and of inputs produced by state-owned enterprises, and a generous public procurement policy that invited corruption.

In the 70s and 80s these instruments were joined by rapidly growing export subsidies, which were intended to compensate for the unfavourable effect of the constantly overvalued exchange rate. The mix of import substitution policies changed repeatedly, without industrial strategy objectives ever playing any part. The conclusion drawn in empirical studies of the effects of these policies on industry is unequivocal: the enterprises derived considerable benefit from protection and subsidies, without coming under internal pressure to make a lasting improvement in their efficiency, productivity and competitiveness.[3] The organizational, technical and social learning processes of the enterprises, permanently underextended because of the constant protection and high subsidies they enjoyed, were slow. Blocked within the domestic market, they tried to minimize risks by diversifying vertically and horizontally. They also developed oligopolistic positions in order to secure further advantages by restricting competition in the domestic market. There was little of the heavy pressure to specialize that is common in industrialized countries and forces enterprises to improve their productivity. "Learning by exporting manufactures" was confined to a small number of enterprises, whose owners and managers mostly came from the last generation of immigrants.

As domestic industrial enterprises were slow to develop, the governments began in the mid-50s to open their economies to foreign direct investors, who soon took over the dynamic, technologically more complex industries. The governments also set up state-owned enterprises in the raw material, intermediate product and capital goods sectors. Faced with the subsidiaries of the foreign corporations and these state-owned enterprises, the domestic private sector saw its opportunities for development dwindle even further. The foreign corporations soon adapted their local plants, which certainly needed no long-term protection, to some of the features of the domestic enterprises.

With their growth prospects increasingly restricted by the small size of the domestic market, the enterprises formed industrial associations, whose main aim was redistribution by government: low taxes, low prices of inputs produced by the state-owned enterprises or the expansion of the public procurement policy. The trade unions' demands were also directed primarily at government. A form of association-based corporatism seeking "redistribution from above" and following on from traditional clientelism emerged. Unlike its counterparts in the German Reich or Japan, it did not pursue industrialization objectives with government, but rather placed excessive trust in its distribution potential, which was in turn determined mainly by exports of raw materials.

As import substitution was constantly and heavily promoted by government and the influence of association-based corporatism grew because the economy was blocked, inflation became chronic. Its main cause was not the inelastic supply of agricultural products or sharply fluctuating export earnings (structuralist thesis), the distribution conflict (neostructuralist thesis) or government's attitude towards revenue and expenditure and thus a lack of budgetary discipline and the consequent rapid growth of the money supply (thesis of the "monetarist" stabilization programmes, which combated the symptom), but rather the allocation of roles to the various protagonists that arose from inward orientation. Inflation was systemic because it could not be combated with enduring success in the given environment of economic policy and power politics, despite a procession of new stabilization programmes. Systemic inflation led to flight into material assets and so to abnormal speculation in real estate.

4   Government as a Distribution Agency: "Industrialization" without a Strategy

Despite growing etatist tendencies, government was by no means trans-formed into a driving force of industrialization. Its autonomy and compe-tence remained extremely limited. It continued to be primarily a distribution agency to the benefit of population groups whose level of organization enabled them to articulate and gain acceptance for their demands. Wide-ranging government interventionism geared to particularist interests did not permit stable regulation, but soon led to chaotic overregulation, which encouraged corruption. It inflated the state bureaucracy, but increasingly restricted the governments' freedom of action in the economic policy sphere. It served short-term interests and stifled individual initiative and market forces generally.

A particular problem was the inability of governments and administrations to reduce the mounting deficits of the state-owned enterprises. Nationalism and nationalization in the raw materials sector in the 60s and 70s led to a decline in investment activity, a drop in this sector's foreign exchange earnings and eventually, in some countries, such as Peru, external borrow-ing by state-owned enterprises that was used solely to finance current government expenditure. However, even governments that were also de-stroying their raw materials base by, among other things, pursuing a clien-telist personnel policy, were simultaneously demanding a New International Economic Order so that they might improve the sales potential of their raw materials and increase their foreign exchange earnings. Here and elsewhere "external factors" were cited to conceal the governments' own weaknesses.

A lack of vision and strategic foresight is indicated by the highly inadequate development of the general and specific environment for industrialization. Governments, administrations and political parties made little attempt at any time to prepare society, or at least the relevant sections of society, for a process of industrialization. They attached little, if any, importance to institutional development; Latin America remained "undermanaged". The public service sector was expanded, but the quality of the health and education systems usually left a great deal to be desired. Research and development was neglected: most enterprises took an interest in it only when it came to adapting imported technologies to domestic conditions and especially to the small domestic market. Government made no attempt to initiate a systematic technological learning process and would have been completely incapable of doing so.

5   Stubborn Adherence to Extensive Growth: Quantity rather than Productivity

What was the main problem faced by industrial development in Latin America or Eastern Europe? It was not the installation of the industrial apparatus, but rather the development of the economic efficiency of industries, once installed, in comparison with those of other countries. The development of productivity was extremely slow at the level of individual enterprises and of the economy as a whole. This was true of the productivity of labour and, increasingly, of capital. With the opportunities for import substitution exhausted, average profitability fell sharply, as evident from US investment in Latin America.[4] By the late 80s it was well below the East and South-East Asian level.

The wealth of easily exportable natural resources permitted extensive growth, which was based on the increasing use of land, labour and capital. This type of growth was in line with the above-mentioned quantitative expansion of the public service sector and the continuing poor quality of social institutions generally. If a process of industrialization is to be dynamic, however, it must be based on increasingly intensive, i.e. productivity- and technology-driven, growth. Such growth is possible only if general conditions are rapidly improved.

Once the industrial import substitution options had been exhausted, investment opportunities for the private sector and its interest in investment soon
dwindled. The import-intensive large-scale government projects launched in
the 70s with considerable external financial backing to improve energy
supplies and expand the primary industry brought no more than a temporary
revival of economic growth. When this situation was joined by a sharp rise
in US interest rates towards the end of the decade, capital flight assumed
massive proportions. Foreign debts soon reached a critical level when
compared with growth prospects. After a number of other anti-inflationary
projects ("heterodox stabilization"), which were doomed to failure and, like
the inflow of capital in the 70s, delayed reorientation, the inward-oriented
approach collapsed in almost all countries of the region in the late 80s or
early 90s, leaving societies without hope.

6   Obstruction of Societal Development by Inward Orientation

It is becoming clear that the many years of excessive inward orientation
have had a profound effect on capitalism in Latin America: its enterprises
have completely different features from their counterparts in the industrialized countries. A state-interventionist macro policy geared to particularist
interests emerged. With the private sector encountering ever greater internal
obstacles, the government sector was increasingly forced to assume responsibility for growth, with which it was, however, less and less able to cope.
Inward orientation also left its mark on the features of social and ecological
development.

1) The assumption that industrial dynamism would trigger constant growth
of domestic demand for manufactures (supply thus creating demand),
without the structural conditions for an increase in this demand having to be
created and improved, proved to be incorrect. The traditional structures of
society disintegrated and were not replaced. As the poor continued to be
poorly organized in almost all the countries, between 30 and 80 per cent of
the population - depending on the country - were unable to gain acceptance
for their interests from the government sector and others in positions of
power. Consequently, they were available neither as independent
democratic actors nor as consumers of manufactures. At elections they gave
their votes to nationalist populists or sometimes even demagogic
conservatives. Domestic demand remained structurally limited ("exclusive

industrialization"). The growth and debt crisis greatly exacerbated the social problems. It is estimated that 183 million people (44 per cent of the total population) were poor in 1990. During the 80s poverty became primarily an urban problem.[5]

2) As in Eastern Europe and India, the low level of productivity in the economy did not permit a significant improvement in the social situation of large sections of the population[6] or, therefore, much of a rise in their level of consumption. Insufficient demand soon killed off the inward-oriented economy, especially in the small and some medium-sized countries of the region. Industrial import substitution in Guatemala and Peru advanced no further than assembly and bottling plants. Vertical social mobility, already unremarkable, was also restricted by the no more than sporadic improvement in supply conditions at the socially relevant pre-competition stage and especially in the training of skilled workers.

3) Inward orientation did very serious damage to the environment. The main cause of pollution in the past was the economy's inefficiency. With little pressure on anyone to rationalize, a dynamic, increasingly structured learning process did not occur. All the inward-oriented economies consequently failed to emerge from the second industrial revolution. It should be noted that, contrary to the view commonly held in the industrialized countries and in Latin America itself, the shortage of capital was by no means the most serious obstacle to development. Given the undoubted waste of capital, which was, in the final analysis, due to the same factors as the boundless waste of energy, the main question that arises is how capital was used during the period of inward orientation. Because of the latter, resource use was not governed by any clear and unequivocal criteria.

7   Neoliberal Economic Policy: Destruction of Old Structures and the First Step towards World-Market-Oriented Specialization

By their own efforts alone the national actors on whom inward orientation had had a formative influence were incapable of realigning economic policy.[7] The change, when it came, was made possible only by the persistent pressure of debt servicing, by the compelling need to accept the IMF's stabilization programmes and the World Bank's adjustment programmes and by the votes of the poor, who rejected the ineffectual inward-oriented actors. Like Eastern Europe, almost all the countries of the region are today pursuing a neoliberal economic policy.

The goal is no longer "industrialization", which had encountered insurmountable internal obstacles and was hardly ever a serious objective of actual economic policy, but the development of a market economy which will create confidence among private enterprises and lead them to increase productivity and exports significantly. Import liberalization, deregulation, the privatization of most state-owned enterprises and a radical reform of the government sector are intended to stabilize and develop macroeconomic conditions, to strengthen market forces and to bring about achievement-oriented competition and - primarily through a heavy commitment by foreign investors - the world-market-oriented specialization of the economies.

In the transition from inward orientation to world market specialization the neoliberal concepts borrowed from the USA have an important, perhaps even essential role to play. In view of the political resistance from the organized forces that not infrequently still dominate the parliaments and the weakness of the new protagonists and of the institutions at their disposal it is unrealistic to assume that there can be a direct transition to complex economic policy guidance of the kind often advocated, especially in Latin America.[8] Neoliberalism enables the inward-oriented power-based network to be destroyed (though not, of course, all the power and wealth structures that have been handed down). It enables a new - in some countries already stable - macro policy to be pursued and a reform that separates government, industry and society to be undertaken, thus paving the way for collaboration between relatively autonomous partners. This is the first fundamental reform of the government sector for five hundred years. Neoliberalism also forces society as a whole to change its values and patterns of behaviour and especially to develop private initiative.

As is only to be expected, the shaping of the new economic order is still far from complete. This is true of price and competition policy, monetary and financial policy, fiscal policy and the strengthening of allocative and growth forces by government, foreign trade policy, wage and labour market policy and legislation to protect the consumer. It is also becoming increasingly apparent that the neoliberal concepts raise major problems: they ignore the fact - known since the late Middle Ages - that without adequate regulation workable markets will not emerge. As these concepts lack an industrial policy dimension, many enterprises that are in principle capable of modern-ization and specialization are forced out of business. And they overlook the fact that willingness to invest and an economy's competitiveness very much depend on the development and consolidation of a new environment for the economy and of general social conditions.

Institutional reform and the development of a new social order are similarly in their infancy in Latin America. Debureaucratization, administrative reform and especially decentralization are encountering major obstacles. If regional and local authority is to be strengthened and the room for financial manoeuvre at these levels increased, a sound relationship between central government and the lower levels of policy-making and administration must first be established. As is particularly apparent from excessive decentraliza-tion in Peru, the efficiency of regional and local government depends not least on the existence of efficient, relatively autonomous central govern-ment. Nor can other aspects of the social environment (fundamental rights, confidence in the legal system, a constitutional judiciary, the participation of intermediary organizations in decision-making processes at the various levels of policy-making and administration, freedom of speech and informa-tion) simply be decreed: they have to be acquired through experience. The stability and quality of democracy are based on a social learning process. Above all, they require a balance of power between government, enterprises and trade unions within the new framework.

Transitional problems are also occurring because the new system of regula-tion is not yet sufficiently developed and performance-stimulating systems of incentives and sanctions are not having the intended effect. The privatization of numerous state-owned enterprises in particular has made it possible to balance national budgets; in Mexico at least and probably in Chile too, privatization has done more to reduce foreign debts than the Brady Plan.[9] Privatization - or preparations for it in Brazil's case - and relatively high interest rates have, however, created a climate that has led to a massive influx of portfolio investment. São Paulo, Buenos Aires, Mexico City and Bogotá have experienced an overheated stock market boom. In some coun-tries, especially Chile and Mexico, foreign direct investment in the pro-ductive sector and particularly in mining and natural-resource-intensive industries and, in Mexico's case, the automobile industry too, is also on the increase. To date there has been no sign of a sharp increase in the region's exports. Imports have recently been rising more quickly than exports.[10]

8   Effects of Reorientation on the Economy

The reorientation of economic policy is having radical effects on the economy:

1) Streamlining at enterprise level shows that only part of the private sector is able to cope with the reform process. There are signs of a radical change in the structure of the business community. Now that the barriers to markets have been removed, the enterprises experiencing growth are mostly those which are contributing to world-market-oriented specialization in mining, agriculture and natural-resource-intensive industries. Many of them, including some state-owned enterprises, are already increasing their productivity significantly. The organizational, technical and social reforms at enterprise level are far from complete; changing the organization of production and work is proving particularly difficult in the technologically more demanding enterprises, especially as even in the industrialized countries the use of "new technologies" is causing uncertainty over the concepts in this sphere.

2) The privatization of numerous state-owned enterprises is strengthening not only - and in some countries not even mainly - the position of foreign corporations but rather the domestic private sector. Only now are large domestic private enterprises emerging, and some of them will probably be capable of occupying world market segments after a period of consolidation and specialization. However, not a few groups of enterprises ("grupos económicos"), encouraged by what they see as favourable privatization projects, are resorting to risky horizontal diversification.

3) The subsidiaries of multinational corporations are being reorganized so that they can be incorporated in the latter's worldwide strategies. This too indicates that only now is one world economy emerging. Thus Mexico, being near to the USA and part of the projected North American Free Trade Zone, has become a far more dynamic automotive centre than Brazil, which has a potentially large domestic market to offer, but one that has failed to develop dynamically for many years.[11]

4) The "integration of industry" has become less important than it once was. Industrial linkages often prove difficult to forge; in an effort to become internationally competitive, industry is introducing technologies and machinery from the industrialized countries on a far larger scale than it used to. A significant proportion of the domestic capital goods industry is being forced

to close down, as was the case in Spain after its accession to the European Community.[12] The aim today is to expand certain production chains, such as the footwear industry in Brazil, a requirement being that all the links in the chain are competitive. An attempt is also being made to create a favourable basis for international competition in new areas of specialization, such as agriculture, fisheries and the wood-processing industry in Chile,[13] by achieving linkage effects and improving the environment for the sectors concerned. Organizational and technical modernization has also begun at the large industrial complexes and especially in the steel and petrochemical industries of Brazil, Mexico, Argentina and Venezuela.[14]

9   Development of a Social Dimension in the Market Economy: First Signs

What social development is likely within the new framework? The most effective means of reducing poverty is a level of economic growth well above that of population growth. After the tax reforms being undertaken everywhere, it would increase fiscal resources and, therefore, the scope for distribution, employment, now even in agriculture, and, gradually, real wages. This is already happening in Chile.

To alleviate rural poverty, an attempt is being made - even in Peru of late - to raise producer prices in the agricultural sector. At the time of inward orientation, when urban-populist interests dominated, they became increasingly depressed.[15] It may be possible in the medium term to increase agricultural production, to reduce the now high level of food imports (subsidized first in the industrialized countries and then again in the importing country) and to strengthen the internal economic circuits. This is one of the major requirements for national integration, especially in the countries with an Indian rural population.

The neoliberal governments also have a number of important social policy concepts, most prompted by the World Bank. They are principally designed to reduce extreme poverty by backing the reorientation of economic policy with special employment programmes and measures for specific target groups in sectors where the social indicators are least favourable.[16]

Greater efforts are also being made to curb population growth, a basic determinant of social development, by improving the conditions relating to access to self-determined family planning. Some countries of the region appear to be succeeding in making the transition from the explosive growth of recent decades to average annual growth of less than 1.5 per cent.[17] This alone will make it possible for the social services (health, education, social housing, transport, energy, drinking water supply, sewage removal, waste disposal) to be expanded sufficiently.

There are also approaches to a radical reform of social policy. In the past social policy primarily benefited the middle classes and did little to combat poverty and improve social conditions for industrialization. A new, less etatist social policy is emerging, especially in Chile and Mexico. The social services (social insurance, schools, hospitals) are being privatized in some cases, decentralized in others. A state social policy with poverty alleviation as its main objective is being formulated. There are also signs of a new education policy, which may help to improve supply conditions by, say, providing skilled workers with a broad training and focusing on science and technology at the universities.

In some countries efforts are already being made to form a social partnership between labour and capital. The government stipulation of minimum wages and minimum working conditions is being phased out. The two sides of industry are being granted the right to free collective bargaining and so to determine wage levels and work norms. However, employers' associations and trade unions, which might act as lobbies, have only begun to mature since they realized there was no future in relying on government to provide for distribution.

Despite such new and important approaches to social policy, the long period of social disintegration will continue if the rules of the free market economy are strictly applied over a long period. Overcoming this disintegration calls for a greater social commitment. Furthermore, as industrialized countries with a "laissez-faire" market economy show, not enough importance is attached to improving the structural conditions for growth, industrialization and international competition. Both problems - the "social question" and the "competition question" - make it essential for the social dimension of the market economy to be developed in the 90s. Strengthening social organization to benefit the poor is very important in this context. It is not only a question of the "technocratic solutions" on which attention is focused at present but also of growing (sometimes far too quickly) "pressure from below".

In the countries of Latin America it is likely to be some time before the political parties and governments make a social commitment to the development of the public institutions needed to alleviate poverty and form human capital and to the achievement of a consensus among the socially, culturally and ideologically divided population on basic social values and objectives; in many ways the circumstances are unfavourable.

10   The Ecological Dimension of the Market Economy: Resource and Environmental Protection Lagging Behind

As deregulation has not been followed by adequate new regulation, the threat to the environment, and especially to the now far more intensively used natural resources, is growing. Chile shows that even diversified natural resources can be quickly exhausted where there is little regulation and the latest technology is used. The almost total absence of control over the exploitation of nature by the private sector, and particularly by Japanese corporations, under the military dictatorship led to the overuse of land, forest and marine resources. Maximum exploitation geared to quick profits resulted in the unjustifiable use of agricultural chemicals, the clearance of many primary forests in the south of the country, overfishing and even higher concentrations of sulphur and arsenic in areas where ores are smelted. The democratic government has begun to change the legal basis and to increase the administrative and technological know-how of the public monitoring agencies.

Chile and Mexico in particular are attempting to prevent a further deterioration of living conditions in the cities, especially Santiago and Mexico City. Some of the problems can certainly be solved in the medium term, others are likely to come to a head in the very near future: for one thing, although population growth is slowing (to 1.9 per cent p.a. from 1985-90), the urban population is growing by 2.8 per cent p.a., which will take it to nearly 400 million by 2000;[18] for another, the car population is increasing rapidly in many countries of the region - with the same effects as this has had in the North.

The development of a resource-conserving, environmentally compatible, secure and economic energy supply system is very important. A sharp increase in the use of natural gas, a fuel with a low pollutant content, can be expected in many countries. Further large reservoirs of the Itaipú or

Yacyretá type are hardly likely to be built in the foreseeable future. Nuclear energy is unlikely to play a major role.

The industrial sector offers considerable scope for the conservation and rational use of raw materials and energy, both through rationalization in the enterprises and the use of machines and technologies that are low consumers of energy and materials and through the recycling of by-products and waste. National environmental protection industries may also become an important growth sector. In agriculture sustainable, resource-preserving land use is a goal that can be achieved only in a lengthy process of reform. The same is true of the preservation of the tropical rainforests and other primary forests.

Although the reorientation of economic policy has been accompanied by a significant increase in willingness to combat or avoid damage to the environment, government and industry are not yet strong and efficient enough to develop and implement a national environmental policy. Countries with a chaotic economic policy, a lack of competence and budget and debt problems will also find it impossible to protect the environment, a link that is not infrequently overlooked by observers from the industrialized countries. Only as economic growth revives will the scope for the protection of resources and the environment increase. The aim must be to concentrate such protection on the most important achievable objectives: new, environmentally oriented regulation that brings about a fundamental change in the legislative framework, the development of efficient monitoring agencies and the promotion of research and advanced training geared to specific environmental problems. Only when a national environmental policy begins to have an impact will the gradual adjustment of resource and environmental protection to internationally recognized standards be possible. This is likely to be the most important goal of environmental policy in the foreseeable future.

The view described above departs from propositions occasionally put forward in industrialized countries that development in the South is reaching "ecological limits" or that the excessive exploitation of the environment in Latin America is closely associated with the continent's integration into the present world market. Environmental degradation in the past was mainly due to poor government control and limited pressure to develop productivity and so to achieve intensive growth. Excessive inward orientation is far more to blame than integration into the world economy. This is not to say that, if the rules of the free market economy are strictly applied over a long period and government therefore remains relatively weak, the forthcoming world-market-oriented specialization will not follow the centuries-old pattern of the ruinous exploitation of natural resources.

There is no indication that the Latin American countries will be innovative enough to develop environmentally friendly technologies and production methods largely by their own efforts. For the environmental compatibility of economic activities, the development of efficient, low-energy communications and transport systems and the greater use of renewable energies the region remains heavily dependent on the North. In all probability only technical innovations and changed life styles in the industrialized countries will make the more rapid development of resource and environmental protection in Latin America possible. World-market-oriented specialization will, after all, provide far more opportunities for adopting problem-solving approaches that have already been put to the test in the industrialized countries. For the foreseeable future, however, Latin America will be even further removed from "desarrollo sustentable"[19] than the industrialized countries.

11   Conclusions on Inward Orientation and Evaluation of the Transition Process

Initially, industrial import substitution led to high economic growth. There was considerable potential for substitution, demand for manufactures increased, government ensured permanent protection and granted high subsidies. Then the potential for substitution was exhausted; the development dynamism of more and more inward-oriented enterprises was obstructed. At the same time nationalists weakened the most important source of foreign exchange, the export of natural resources, by nationalizing foreign enterprises. In most cases, this was followed by a rapid loss of efficiency.

The compromises in power politics and economic policy that made industrial import substitution possible and drove it on nurtured government interventionism, stifled market forces in many sectors. However, while this and the obstruction of enterprises resulted in the inexorable growth of demands that the government sector ensure economic growth, association-based corporatism, increasingly geared to distribution, was fragmenting this sector. It was this corporatism, not neoliberalism as often assumed, that eventually destroyed the government sector. Within the inward-oriented framework the governments had only one option left: large-scale projects, stabilization programmes and foreign borrowing.

In the absence of empirical studies the effects of government interventionism on the economy long remained a closed book. It was only when the government actors and their instruments collapsed that it was discovered how badly the criterion of efficient resource use had been neglected. The main problem in any development process, not just industrialization, i.e. acquiring national organizational, technical and social competence, was not perceived by the protagonists in Latin America until the 70s and 80s. Prior to this the demands that progress in the industrialized countries made on their own societies were also overlooked.

As inward-oriented investment lost its attraction for domestic and foreign industrial enterprises, the credit and financial system loosened its ties with the productive sector. The radical, but half-hearted neoliberal concepts, especially the fight against inflation by the "monetary approach to the balance of payments", that were implemented in the latter half of the 70s, particularly in the Cono Sur, resulted in deregulation, which enabled the bankers and industrialists, blocked within the inward-oriented framework, to become financial speculators.[20] In the 70s flight capital was often replaced with foreign credits on what seemed to be favourable terms. From the late 70s massive capital flight was accompanied by a rapidly growing foreign debt.

Inward orientation led to societal introspection. The intelligentsia had eyes only for exogenous causes of dependence and underdevelopment. It blamed the "system" and "third parties". Promising industrialization strategies have yet to be formulated in the region. There was no "catching up" in "inward-oriented industrialization" because it excluded the productivity dimension and the quality of social development. Despite this, reference is not infrequently made today to the "failure of catch-up industrialization".

Latin America's growth and debt crisis has not yet been overcome by any means. In almost every country the government and administration are still "weak actors"; this is especially true as regards the demands emanating from the poor sections of the population and the impoverished middle classes, the "new technologies" and fierce international competition. If it is forgotten that the transition is a process, if no account is taken of the growing signs of a more rapid learning process in industry, government and society in a number of countries, it can be said - even by neoliberals - that the attempt to liberalize the economy has failed. Particularly where economic growth is concerned, cautious optimism is more appropriate, although it does not, of course, extend to all countries.

Setbacks are inevitable: they will be caused by the unfavourable internal conditions, and especially by the power and economic elites in not a few countries who have no interest in social development, by weak social organizations and by inefficient public institutions; and they will also be caused by the protectionism of the industrialized countries and their reluctance to do more than make various recommendations and conditions and actually commit themselves to the reorientation of economic and social policy in Latin America. This is particularly true of a significant reduction in foreign debts, financial and technical participation in emergency social funds, even in Peru, and support from development cooperation for the formation of structures within the new framework.[21] Setbacks are very likely to occur in some small and medium-sized countries. Their capacity for development is often limited; they can have little hope at present of benefiting from the rapid growth of large countries in the region.

12   "Conservatism of Unconcern": The Shortcomings of Economic Policy and Crisis in the Social System

With the collapse of inward orientation, neoclassical ways of thinking and economic policies based on the conception of the absolute individuality and uniqueness of economic problems and their solutions are gaining ground in many countries of the world. Three decades ago Ralf Dahrendorf accused "modern sociology", where it presupposed "a balanced, functioning social system" and thus rejected a "conflict model of society", of "conservatism of unconcern", which was admittedly "implicit" and not, therefore, "militant like that of a Raymond Aron ... or a Milton Friedman."[22]

As its own economic policy options have been exhausted, Latin America is today dominated by a form of the free market economy which has triggered a carefree lack of regulation and guidance in all sectors of society. Wherever it is pursued, neoliberal economic policy of the American type shows an absence of concern for three of the principal social problems: firstly, the development of the national competition base, on which the international competitiveness of industry is increasingly based today; secondly, social development, and especially the problem of extreme poverty; thirdly, the relationship between economics and ecology. This is true of the Latin American countries despite the important new approaches in the areas of economic, social and environmental policy.

1) Although they played an important role in the process of radical change, "market and free trade" in the long term represent a further "soft option" with respect to the requirements of dynamic industrial specialization, social development and minimizing pollution. The free market economy is not an adequate response to the economic, financial, organizational, technical, social and ecological problems of societies in serious crisis. In much the same way as India, Algeria, the Eastern European countries, China and some capitalist industrialized countries, Latin America has just begun the search for appropriate economic and social policies and industrialization strategies, which consists of various sequences.[23]

The nationalist, etatist and anti-business structuralism of the Latin American type, which spawned economically unproductive hybrids of "market and plan", cannot be replaced with a quickly designed form of neostructuralism, as some Latin American intellectuals appear to assume.[24] This is not to say that pragmatic neostructuralism may not have some relevance in the future as an alternative to the now dominant neoliberalism, but it must then assign a central role to the private sector, provide for a relatively autonomous government sector and efficient public institutions, heed the call for technical learning to develop the "technical culture" and for the acquisition of know-how relating to the world economy, emphasize the role of a financial system geared to the needs of the productive sector and take account of the important link between the degree of social organization and the ability of domestic actors to play a guiding role.

A vision, which might be transformed into a strategy, of how the export of natural resources and natural-resource-based manufactures might be joined by industrial specialization and eventually even a process of organizational and technical catching up and the market economy made socially and ecologically more compatible once the transitional phase has been completed does not yet exist in the Latin American countries. The competence and bargaining power of the domestic actors and the efficiency of the institutions at their disposal are still far from equal to the task of simply shaping the economic policy framework in such a way that industrial specialization strategies similar to those of East and South-East Asian countries can be implemented.

2) The unconcerned conservatism on which American neoliberalism is based is particularly inappropriate because the countries that were inward-oriented in the past now face a serious social crisis: strict adherence to the rules of the free market economy will further accelerate the process of social disintegration which is well advanced under state capitalism and state socialism. Economic growth and the emerging new social policy cannot resolve the "social question" on their own. Instead, government must make a far greater contribution to the alleviation of poverty than it has hitherto: by undertaking structural reforms, especially in the agricultural sector, implementing programmes of direct poverty alleviation, supporting the organization of poor population groups and purposefully improving conditions for growth, competitiveness and industrialization.

The aim must be to create national markets, which have so far failed to emerge in such countries as Peru and Guatemala owing to the absence of social integration, gradually to increase domestic demand for manufactures and to support the development of intermediary organizations and thus an improvement in the conditions for democratic participation. Amitai Etzioni has criticized neoliberalism for failing to appreciate that workable markets form part of "a moral and social context".[25] This context, however, is still undeveloped in Latin America. Despite the reorientation of economic policy, the diffuse "pressure from below" that is due to social disintegration, accumulated social pressure and stifled expectations is growing by the year. This pressure is also being exploited by undemocratic forces and is already threatening to exceed the formal democratic limits in such countries as Peru and Venezuela.[26]

With the transition the internal and external pressure for dynamic industrial specialization is quickly rising. The population of the region is expected to grow from 437 million in 1990 to 529 million in 2000 and 737 million in 2025.[27] Mass production is essential if the poor and the middle classes are to enjoy even a minimum of prosperity. Unless the domestic capacity for transformation grows extremely quickly in this situation, not a few countries of Latin America will sink in chaos.

History is open-ended; only what will undoubtedly be a lengthy process of trial, error and adjustment will show whether Latin American and Eastern European countries are capable of overcoming the many different problems that stand in the way of dynamic industrialization and broad social development by forming national and regional structures and of developing a complex system of overall guidance by independent, yet collaborating groups of private and public actors at various levels of policy-making and administration and in the various sections of society.

13   Requirements to be Met by the Latin American Countries (I): the Relationship between Domestic, Regional and World Demand: "Both-And" rather than "Either-Or"

During the strategy and debt crisis of the 80s domestic demand largely collapsed; real wages, for example, were halved or even quartered. This and the need to find a way out of the external economic trap make a substantial increase in exports of goods and services essential.[28] The aim should be not, as recommended by the World Bank at one time, "outward oriented ... trade strategies"[29] but to make the world market the frame of reference for the economy. Exports should rise at least to a level that enables imports of machinery to be increased despite debt servicing. In many cases, this alone will permit a significant improvement in international competitiveness.

Protectionism will, however, prevent the export of most manufactures to the North as a long-term proposition. Rising domestic demand is therefore very important if unemployment is to be significantly reduced, poverty alleviated and the dynamism of growth sustained. As Porter emphasizes,[30] differentiated domestic demand is also a major requirement for international competitiveness. Nor can exports of manufactures to the industrialized countries be sustained at a very high level. Closer regional cooperation and integration is therefore very important. In the past subregional integration was used principally to increase the scope for industrial import substitution. Several free trade zones and at least one integration project (MERCOSUR) are now emerging with such new aims as a joint improvement in supply and demand conditions.[31]

14   Requirements (II): Development of Pre-Competitive Structures

Within the new framework central government, the regions and local authorities have the task of improving the conditions for the world-market-oriented specialization and international competitiveness of the economy. Initially, the emphasis is on the export-oriented expansion of the physical infrastructure (roads, railways, ports, telecommunications), which has the backing of the World Bank and the Inter-American Development Bank (IDB). The competitiveness of the economy depends above all on whether a pre-competition sector can be quickly established, the main aim being the development of national technological competence.

The effectiveness and intensity of technology transfer has so far been impaired primarily by the low level and extremely slow development of technological competence at enterprise and government level. Technological competence means knowing what technologies are available and being able to assess them, to select the one that is most appropriate, to use, adapt and improve it and eventually to develop technologies oneself. This competence is today the most important requirement for socio-economic development, industrial specialization and international competitiveness.[32] It must be developed in such way that a national system of innovation emerges.

National technological competence stems from an efficient education system. Vocational schools and universities where the emphasis is on science and technology are particularly relevant in this context. The development of technology-oriented institutions (weights and measures, standardization, testing, quality assurance, patent protection, R&D centres and financing, technology transfer) is very important. It is essential for technological institutions to be highly user-oriented. Innovativeness should be especially encouraged in small and medium-sized firms. Government can and must contribute to the emergence of a national technological community capable of coordinating technology-related activities through "national dialogues".[33] An innovation-oriented national competition strategy can only be developed gradually, as strong actors emerge at enterprise and government level and in the third sector.

15 The New Challenge: Formation of Structures, Joint Problem-Solving, National Dialogue, Systemic Competitiveness

The restructuring of enterprises and associations and the establishment of a pre-competition sector are two of the first steps to be taken in the development of the "national competitive advantage".[34] The new challenge facing the countries of Latin America calls for an approach to the creation of systems that is geared to the formation of structures in all sectors of relevance to competition, the pooling of national forces wherever this seems possible and a continuous dialogue among the various domestic actors. The following five requirements, which should be satisfied by any country trying to achieve dynamic industrial development, must be borne in mind:

1) Industrial specialization and social development call for intensive "learning from others", to which considerable importance has been attached in Europe and East Asia. It consists mainly of organizational, technical and social learning from economies with high levels of productivity, not by simply copying their advantages but by imitating them creatively. Independent technical and social development requires an institutionalized learning process that extends to the whole of society.

2) Macro policy is relatively independent, something that was overlooked at the time of inward orientation. It cannot be instrumentalized to further political and social aims. Its main task is to ensure low rates of inflation and as balanced an exchange rate as possible.

3) The exploitation of existing locational advantages does not as a rule permit a significant and, above all, sustained increase in exports. In all sectors, including those producing primary goods, most competitive positions are "man-made" today. They are created by enterprises which seek, under pressure from international competition, to achieve the organizational and technical standards usual in their sector. The dynamic enterprises in Latin America are already complementing their internal rationalization efforts with cooperation among themselves, by forming export consortia, for example. The private sector's interest in the development of the pre-competition sector is also growing. However, the industrial enterprises still have a long way to go before they rise to the level of imitative innovation and rapid commercialization for which East Asia is renowned.

4) If significant advances are to be made in productivity - and this is likely to be possible only in a world-market-oriented economy - it is essential, on the one hand, to expose enterprises to pressure of competition that they can withstand while modernizing and specializing and yet, on the other hand, to support the economy's international competitiveness with government contributions to the development of the "national competitive advantage" For this it is very important to develop structures at the level between macroeconomic conditions and micro actors ("meso level"). Structuring the meso dimensions[35] must be accompanied by a pooling of forces through ever closer cooperation among the various levels of policy-making and administration, industrial associations, trade unions and the now fast

growing third sector. The aim is to develop close relationships and flexible networks of the various actors, to improve national bargaining power and to establish a complex system of guidance.

5) After a long and heated debate on economic policy it is agreed today that general market and competition orientation, a stable macro framework and goal-oriented, interlocking measures at macro, meso and micro level are essential if internationally competitive industries are to be developed. Another view that is hardly disputed is that it is important for there to be a "national dialogue" on the aims of industrialization and the instruments used to achieve them. In contrast, the contribution that selective policies (on the promotion of specific sectors, groups of enterprises and technologies, selective export promotion and selective protection of imports) should make to strengthening the international competitiveness of industry is an issue on which opinions continue to differ widely.

Recent studies have concluded that, like Japan, the Republic of Korea has succeeded in combining market forces with strategic planning and selective intervention and so in facilitating adjustment processes at enterprise level.[36] Selective industrial and trade policies, however, have an indispensable role to play only when an attempt is made in industrially backward countries to advance into the technology-intensive growth sectors of the world economy. In Latin America this attempt has so far been made only by small groups of enterprises. It must be assumed that in the 90s foreign trade policy in the industrially advanced countries of the region will vacillate between the neo-liberal "pure open-economy strategy" and a more complex "selective integration strategy", depending on the ability of national actors to establish strategies and on the aims of their respective industrial policies.[37]

Notes

1   See **K. Esser**, Perú. Una salida de la crisis, GDI, Berlin, June 1989, p. 4.

2   See **B. Kosacoff / J. Todesca / A.** Vispo, La transformación de la industria automotriz argentina - su integración con Brasil, CEPAL-Oficina en Buenos Aires, July 1992.

3   For example, **K. Esser et al.**, Monetarismus in Uruguay - Wirkungen auf den Industriesektor, GDI, Berlin 1983; **T. Kampffmeyer et al.**, Nichttraditionelle Exporte Kolumbiens. Eine Analyse von Erfolgsfällen, GDI, Berlin 1986.

4   The **Institute of International Finance, Inc.**, Fostering Foreign Direct Investment in Latin America, Washington, D.C., 1990, p. 8, Table 7; in 1990 GDP was, at US $ 946 billion, above that of East Asia (excluding Japan) and the Pacific region (US $ 939 billion) (per capita: US $ 2,180 vs US $ 600); value added in manufacturing industry (in US $ billion at current value) in 1989: Brazil 120.8 and Mexico 51.1 (China 145.6; Republic of Korea 66.2; India 44.4) (World Bank, World Development Report 1992, Washington, D.C., 1992, p. 196, Table A.2, and p. 228, Table 6); indicators of this kind say little about the quality of an industrialization process.

5   In 1950 60 per cent of Latin Americans lived in rural areas, in 1990 30 per cent; in 1970 37 per cent of the poor lived in urban areas, in 1980 46 per cent and in 1986 56 per cent (CEPAL, Nota sobre el desarrollo social en América Latina, Santiago de Chile, July 1991, pp. 4 and 17).

6   Some important social indicators certainly improved in relative terms: life expectancy at birth: 51.8 years from 1950-55, 66.7 years from 1985-90; infant mortality (per 1,000 live births): 127.7 vs 59.8; illiteracy (per cent of population aged 15 or older): 44.0 vs 15.3; per cent of poor households: 1970 40.0, 1985-1990 37.0 (CEPAL, Social Equity and Changing Production Patterns: an Integrated Approach, CEPAL News, May 1992); in absolute terms, however, the poor and also the extremely poor population grew in not a few countries; the social indicators do not take account of the quality of provision in the health and education sectors, for example; in many countries the social situation of the population has deteriorated seriously since 1982; thus "malnutrición temprana" (up to the age of 5) causes permanent damage in 64 per cent of children in the southern highlands of Peru and in 46 per cent of children throughout Peru (according to studies carried out by the Escuela de Administración de Negocios para Graduados/ESAN, Lima, in the late 80s and early 90s).

7   For the difficulties encountered in reorienting economic policy in the 80s see **K. Esser (ed.)**, Argentinien. Zum industriepolitischen Suchprozess seit 1983, GDI, Berlin, March 1989.

8   For example, **S. Bitar / C.I. Bradford, Jr.**, Strategic Options for Latin American Trade in the 90s, Inter-American Development Bank/OECD Development Centre, working paper, 1991.

9   See **P. Tandon et al.**, Mexico, Vol. 1, Background, TELMEX, Vol. 2, AERO-MEXICO, MEXICANA, World Bank Conference on the Welfare Consequences of Selling Public Enterprises. Case Studies from Chile, Malaysia, Mexico and the U.K., Washington, D.C., 11 and 12 June 1992; foreign debts totalled US $ 373.4 billion in 1984 and US $ 426 billion in 1991 (CEPAL, Balance preliminar de la economía de América Latina y el Caribe 1991, Santiago, 18 December 1991, p. 38, Table 1); forecast by the IDB until 2000: +12 per cent to US $ 461 billion.

10   Regional exports: US $ 121.7 billion in 1990, US $ 122.2 billion in 1991; imports: US $ 92.5 in 1990, US $ 110.3 billion in 1991 (CEPAL, Balance ..., op. cit., p. 38, Table 1); the trade balance surplus thus fell from US $ 29.2 billion to US $ 11.9 billion; 1991 export index (1980 = 100): Latin America 138, Paraguay 320, Chile 188, Brazil 159, Haiti 58; trend in the regional terms of trade in the 80s: -27 per cent (CEPAL).

11   As an exporter of automobile products, Mexico already led Brazil in 1988 (ranking 13th and 14th in the world), its share of world exports being 1.5 per cent compared with

Brazil's 1 per cent (GATT, International Trade 88-89, Vol. 2, Geneva 1989, p. 63, Table IV.56).

12 For the waning importance of Argentina's capital goods industry see **G. Bezchinsky**, Importaciones de bienes de capital. La experiencia argentina en la década del ochenta, CEPAL-Oficina en Buenos Aires, August 1991; for that of the "actividad metalmecánica" (metal-processing industry, including engineering) see **R. Bisang / M. Fuchs / B. Kosacoff**, Internacionalización y desarrollo industrial: Inversiones extranjeras directas de empresas industriales argentinas, CEPAL-Oficina en Buenos Aires, February 1992, p. 41; its share of industrial value added fell sharply: from 28.9 per cent in 1980 to 17.8 per cent in 1990 in Argentina; from 24.8 per cent to 21.5 per cent in Brazil; from 18.9 per cent to 12.4 per cent in Chile; from 21.3 per cent to 21.0 per cent in Mexico (CEPAL, Anuario Estadístico de América Latina y el Caribe, Santiago 1991, pp. 96 f., Table 61).

13 **D. Messner et al.**, Weltmarktorientierung und Aufbau von Wettbewerbsvorteilen in Chile. Das Beispiel der Holzwirtschaft, GDI, Berlin 1991.

14 For the economy's reaction see **D. Messner**, Von der Importsubstitution zur weltmarktorientierten Spezialisierung - Optionen für den Industriesektor Uruguays, GDI, Berlin, March 1990; **J. Meyer-Stamer**, From Import Substitution to International Competitiveness - Brazil's Informatics Industry at the Crossroads, GDI, Berlin, March 1990; **G. Ashoff et al.**, Industrielle Anpassung im Zuge aussenwirtschaftlicher Liberalisierung in Venezuela am Beispiel ausgewählter Branchen, GDI, Berlin 1990; **J. Meyer-Stamer et al.**, Comprehensive Modernization on the Shop Floor: A Case Study of the Brazilian Machinery Industry, GDI, Berlin 1991.

15 Despite the agricultural reform, which was admittedly very inefficient, and despite numerous foreign development projects in the agricultural sector, Peru's inward-oriented agriculture collapsed because producer prices fell ever lower; index of relative prices in the agricultural sector (1950 = 100) 1988: 30 (J. Caller S., Política económica y desarrollo productivo. Un análisis retrospectivo, INP/GTZ, Lima, May 1990, Annex, Table 16).

16 See **K. Esser**, Bundesrepublik Deutschland - Chile: entwicklungspolitische Zusammenarbeit, GDI, Berlin, January 1990, pp. 8 f.; **W. McGreevey**, Social Security in Latin America. Issues and Options for the World Bank, World Bank Discussion Papers, No. 110, Washington, D.C., 1990.

17 For example, Chile: 1980 - 1990 1.7 per cent, 1989 - 2000 1.3 per cent; Brazil 2.2 per cent vs 1.7 per cent; Colombia 2.0 vs 1.5 per cent; Dominican Republic 2.2 per cent vs 1.6 per cent (World Bank, World Development Report 1992, pp. 268 f., Table 26).

18 In 1990 71.9 per cent of Latin America's total population was urban (Venezuela 87.5 per cent, Argentina 86.2 per cent, Uruguay 86.1 per cent, Chile 85.1 per cent, Brazil 76.9 per cent) (CEPAL, Nota sobre el desarrollo social ..., op. cit., p. 7, Table 3); 20.8 million people lived in the region's 12 largest cities in 1950, 84.0 million in 1985 (119.1 million in 2000) (CEPAL, La CEPAL y los asentamientos humanos: desarrollo urbano y equidad, Notas sobre la economía y el desarrollo, Santiago de Chile, June 1988, p. 1).

19 See **CEPAL**, El desarrollo sustentable. Transformación productiva, equidad y medio ambiente, Santiago de Chile 1991.

20 See **K. Esser et al.**, Monetarismus in Uruguay ..., op. cit., pp. 19-23.

21 **GDI**, Entwicklungszusammenarbeit mit Lateinamerika, Berlin, 19 August 1991; **K. Esser**, Neuorientierung in Lateinamerika - Anforderungen an die deutsche EZ der 90er Jahre, working paper, Berlin, March 1992.

22 **R. Dahrendorf**, Pfade aus Utopia. Zu einer Neuorientierung der soziologischen Analyse, in: H. Albert (ed.), Theorie und Umwelt. Ausgewählte Aufsätze zur Wissenschaftslehre der Sozialwissenschaften, Tübingen 1964, pp. 331-350, pp. 346 f., p. 344.

23 **K. Esser**, Development of a Competitive Strategy: A Challenge to the Countries of Latin America in the 90s, GDI, Berlin, September 1991, pp. 10-15.

24   O. Sunkel / G. Zuleta, Neoestructuralismo versus neoliberalismo en los anos noventa, Revista de la CEPAL, No. 42, Santiago, December 1990, pp. 37-53.

25   See N. Piper, Moral schlägt Profit, in: Die Zeit, Vol. 47, 1992, No. 16, p. 31.

26   See K. Esser, Latin America: Some Comments on Economic and Political Transition, in: Economics. A Biannual Collection of Recent German Contributions to the Field of Economic Science, Vol. 43, Tübingen 1991, pp. 107-127, p. 125.

27   CEPAL, Anuario ..., op. cit., pp. 166 f., Table 104.

28   Ratio of exports to output: average for the region 21.6 per cent, Brazil 13.5 per cent, Mexico 22.6 per cent, Argentina 23.1 per cent, Costa Rica 53.8 per cent (CEPAL, Anuario ..., op. cit., p. 74, Table 43).

29   World Bank, World Development Report 1987, Washington, D.C., 1987, p. 78.

30   M.E. Porter, The Competitive Advantage of Nations, New York 1990, pp. 86-100.

31   See K. Esser, Lateinamerika. Welt- und Regionalmarktorientierung. Empfehlungen zur regionalen Kooperation und Integration, Occasional Papers of the GDI, Vol. 98, Berlin 1990.

32   J. Meyer-Stamer, Technologie in der Entwicklungszusammenarbeit, working paper, GDI, Berlin, December 1991.

33   Development Assistance Committee/OECD, The Role of Science and Technology in Development Co-operation with the Less-Advanced Developing Countries in the 90s, Paris, 20 November 1990; see C. Dahlman, Building Technological Capability in Developing Countries and the Role of the World Bank, working paper, 8 January 1990.

34   M.E. Porter, The Competitive Advantage ..., op. cit.

35   K. Esser, Development of a Competitive Strategy ..., op. cit., pp. 15-20.

36   See W. Hillebrand, Industrielle und technologische Anschlußstrategien in teilindustrialisierten Ländern. Bewertung der allokationstheoretischen Kontroverse und Schlussfolgerungen aus der Fallstudie Republik Korea, Occasional Papers of the GDI, Vol. 100, Berlin 1991; idem, Technological Modernization in Small and Medium Industries in Korea. With Special Emphasis on the Role of International Enterprise Cooperation, GDI, Berlin 1992.

37   K. Esser, Development of a Competitive Strategy ..., op. cit., pp. 20-27.

Shaping Industrial Competitiveness in Chile The Case of the Chilean Wood-processing Industry

Dirk Messner

1   Reorientation of Development Strategies in Latin America

The Latin American debate on development strategies is gradually leading to a consensus that the development model of protected inward-oriented industrialization (industrialization through import substitution), which dominated the region for decades, has proved unsound. With the small size of domestic markets preventing growth beyond a certain point and excessively high tariff barriers erected for indefinite periods excluding the pressure of external competition, the gap between Latin American and international productivity levels steadily widened, making it impossible to achieve the original goal of gradual integration into the world economy. The internal crisis factors were further exacerbated by world economic trends (e.g. the decline in the prices of raw materials, high interest rates in the early 80s). The Latin American countries have consequently been overtaken by a comprehensive "model crisis". It is agreed today that patterns of development which ignore the world economy are doomed to failure. Practicable methods of becoming part of the world economy and concepts for developing competitive economies are therefore being sought.[1] The economic policy being pursued as the Latin American economies make the transition from excessive inward orientation to the world economy is essentially determined by neoliberal policy models. The liberalization of foreign trade and the deregulation policies are leading - in Mexico and Argentina, for example - to the erosion of the traditional development model and exposing the national economies to international competition.

2   How does Competitiveness Arise?

The neoliberal view is that outward orientation and general liberalization should result in efficient factor allocation and thus in the formation of competitive economic structures. The neoliberal school concentrates on incentives rather than structural factors and ends up with policy recommendations that are generally in the "get prices right" mould. The adjustment and learning processes needed for the creation of competitive advantages at the level of enterprises, institutions and infrastructure and the support they might receive are not therefore singled out for discussion a priori from this angle. The following adopts a position opposed to this simplistic view of how the market works. It is accepted that the inward orientation of their industries led the Latin American countries into a development cul-de-sac, thus making orientation towards the world market as a frame of reference and efforts to establish competitive economies unavoidable.[2] It is shown, however, that the challenge of achieving industrial competitiveness is not adequately covered by the categories of textbook economics and cannot be met with entirely "market-neutral" macro policies. As Lall puts it: "It is certainly better to get prices right than wrong, but it is a necessary condition for industrial success and not a sufficient one."[3]

If active strategies for integration into the world market are to be developed in Latin America on the basis of sound technology and industrial policies, some fundamental questions, treated as a "black box" by neoliberal theoreticians with a reference to the ingenuity of the market and to the dynamic Schumpeterian entrepreneur, need to be asked: how do competitive advantages in fact arise, what are their essential determinants, and how does sustained competitiveness that is not based on absolute cost advantages (e.g. low wages, favourable resource endowment) develop?

Chile's rapidly growing wood-working industry will be taken as an example in the discussion of these questions.[4] Chile is an interesting case because as early as 1973 the military dictatorship began to pursue a radical strategy of outward orientation, which led to the destruction of the traditional development model, whereas the first steps in this orientation towards the world economy are only now being taken in most Latin American countries. After a difficult "streamlining process", which exacted a heavy social and ecological toll, and the collapse of many inefficient industrial sectors the development of the Chilean economy has looked very promising since the mid-80s.[5] The driving forces in the country's development are a number of export-oriented, natural-resource-intensive sectors which have specialized in certain products (world-market-oriented areas of specialization). After a development sequence characterized primarily by an increase in exports of raw materials and products of the initial stages of processing, the country now faces the challenge of placing industrial competitiveness on a wider footing. Chile is thus a "model case", a country that has already completed what others may have yet to begin.[6]

The wood-processing industry is worth considering for two reasons:

-   **Firstly,** it is a natural-resource-based sector, and it must be assumed that, given the limited efficiency of their industries, the majority of Latin American countries will similarly take the first step towards world-market-oriented specialization in raw-materials-intensive sectors of the economy which need to be modernized.

-   **Secondly,** the Chilean wood-working industry reveals, on the one hand, that natural-resource-intensive sectors too have considerable potential for growth and modernization and, on the other hand, how difficult it is even in this apparently uncomplicated sector to make the transition from the production and export of labour-intensive and largely unprocessed products to manufactures with a higher value added and to achieve and improve sustained competitiveness.

The analytical background to our study is the heuristic concept of *systemic or structural competitiveness*. This approach

-   is designed, on the one hand, to extend the debate on the international competitiveness of individual enterprises to include an analysis of their competitive strength in the context of efficient institutions and a suitable macroeconomic environment. It also considers the development of the **international competitiveness of economies**, which cannot be seen as a simple aggregation of the rankings of enterprises in international markets;

-   examines, on the other hand, unlike the standard static textbook models, not only the given structure of comparative advantages and disadvantages but above all how they develop and become more dynamic. The **learning processes** which the actors and institutions concerned undergo and which underlie the development of competitive advantages are analysed. This view also implies that, though necessary, stable macro policies which facilitate outward orientation are not enough for the development of international competitiveness.

In a report for the OECD Chesnais summarizes this dynamic and systemic view of competitiveness as follows:

"We recognise the international competitiveness of national economies as being built on the competitiveness of the firms which operate within, and export from, its boundaries, but it identifies the competitiveness of national economies as being something more than a simple result of the collective or 'average' competitiveness of its firms. We propose the notion of 'structural competitiveness' as a way of expressing the fact that, while the competitiveness of firms will obviously reflect successful management practice by entrepreneurs or corporate executives, it will also stem from the strength and efficiency of a national economy's productive structure, its technical infrastructure and the other factors determining the externalities on which firms can build."[7]

Determinants of international competitiveness

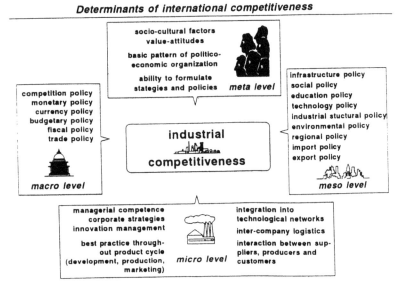

(C) W.Hillebrand / D.Messner / J.Meyer-Stamer, GDI

This concept overcomes one-dimensional approaches to an explanation and refers to the complexity of determinants of international competitiveness. The factors that influence industrial competitiveness form a complex system. The diagram[8] attempts to structure this wide range of determinants of international competitiveness. If competitiveness is to develop, stable economic policies that can be anticipated by the various parties concerned are needed at **macro level**. Competitiveness emerges and is developed in enterprises that are under the pressure of competition and also develop forms of an inter-company division of labour and cooperation, which are becoming increasingly important (**micro level**). Sustainable competitiveness and the establishment of competitive structures depend on specific sectoral policies of private or public institutions (**meso level**) to optimize external economies (e.g. policies on infrastructure, technology and training), to ensure the sustainability of industrial development (environmental policy) and to guarantee social stability and the creativity of employees (social policies). In the final analysis, economic development and thus competitiveness form part of politico-social systems (**meta level**), although unequivocal causal relationships cannot be established here.[9] This "schematic fresco" for approximating the phenomenon of industrial competitiveness requires the backing of empirical evidence if the relative weighting of the various influences is to be determined.[10]

The following chapters primarily concern trends at micro level (Chapter III.1 and 2) and changes in the relationship between employers' and employees' organizations (meta level, Chapter III.3) as the transition is made from inward to world market orientation and competitiveness emerges. It becomes clear that "catch-up modernization" in the area of structural policy (meso level) and a flexible and constructive interplay of entrepreneurial, government and trade union actors and institutions (Chapter IV) are needed in the Chilean wood-processing industry to accelerate the emergence of technology-based competitiveness.

3   The Chilean Forest Industries Sector

With output valued at well over US $ 1 billion (1991), the Chilean forest industries sector[11] accounts for slightly more than 3.5 per cent of the country's gross national product. It employs some 3 per cent of the total labour force, or 80,000 people. The role it plays in the economy is more clearly revealed by its contribution to the country's export earnings, for whose favourable trend it has been largely responsible since outward orientation began. While timber and cellulose exports accounted for only 3.8 per cent of total exports in 1970, the figure had risen to about 10 per cent by the early 90s. These relative figures conceal a tenfold increase in production over this period.[12] Exports rose from about US $ 40 million in 1973 to US $ 850 million in 1991. Some 90 per cent of the raw material handled by the wood-processing industry originates from forestry plantations (currently 1.2 million ha), only 10 per cent from the remaining natural forests. As the timber potential of the plantations will approximately triple by 2010, a concept of sustainable forest management is conceivable in Chile provided that the government enforces effective protection of the natural forest.[13]

Government-subsidized afforestation programmes aside, there have been no specific sectoral policies. The dynamism of the development of the forest industries sector is thus essentially due to macro policies that promote exports and to the enterprises' own dynamism.

Two phases of development are discernible in the Chilean forest industries sector between 1974/75 and 1991, after it had been inward-oriented and far from dynamic in its development until the mid-70s:

-    With Chile's outward orientation there began in 1974/75 an extensive export phase, which featured high growth rates. This upward trend was largely due to exports of such natural-resource-intensive products as round and sawn timber and cellulose. Absolute cost advantages gained from the natural availability of timber resources (forest growth well above the average), the sharp rise in timber potential due to go- vernment-subsidized afforestation programmes (since the 60s) and low labour, transport and environmental costs, together with a macro policy that encouraged exports (devaluation of the national currency, reduction of import duties, withdrawal of foreign exchange restrictions), formed the basis of the sector's dynamic development and its international com- petitiveness (factor-driven development). According to World Bank calculations, production costs (from the cost of afforestation to the cost of transport to the export terminals) for logs of the most important species in Chile, Pinus radiata, are only 30 to 50 per cent of costs at such production locations as the USA and the Scandinavian countries, which compete directly with Chile's timber suppliers in the world market.[14] A few large enterprises accounted for the bulk of export revenues during this "easy export phase".

-   After a serious crisis in the early 80s the forest industries sector stagnated until the middle of the decade. Since 1986 there has been a new, dynamic growth phase, accompanied by heavy investments.[15] The value of the sector's output (excluding furniture) increased from US $ 492 million in 1985 to about US $ 1.2 billion in 1991, export revenues in the same period rising from US $ 326 million to about US $ 850 million. Two trends are important in this context: firstly, traditional natural-resource-intensive products continue to be largely responsible for the dynamism of growth, but their quality is being significantly improved, which is already leading to an increase in domestic value added. Secondly, the **processing** of available timber resources is expanding, and the sawn timber, furniture, board and paper subsectors are diversifying their products. Exports of non-traditional products (e.g. veneers, packaging materials and furniture) and new investment in these subsectors have been rising sharply since the mid-80s (factor-creating and investment-driven development).

In the past five years the domestic market has absorbed a stable share of 30 per cent of the output of the forest industries sector in value terms, which means that it has developed just as dynamically as the trend in exports. There has been considerable **diversification of export markets**. By the late 80s the Chilean wood-working industry was exporting to 58 countries (compared with about 40 in the early 80s). Owing to the persistent economic crisis the importance of what was the leading market until the early 80s, Latin America, has waned, while exports to Europe, Asia and even the USA have risen sharply.[16]

The available literature has had little to say on the features underlying these macro figures of the growth and modernization process towards industrialization at enterprise level and changes in the business environment or on the initiators of this structural change. Clearly, the dynamic development in the highly natural-resource-intensive sectors (cellulose, round timber, sawn timber) was due to heavy investment by the large enterprises in these subsectors. Product diversification and the export of new products also seemed - from an analysis of the available material - to be largely due to investment by larger enterprises.

As, however, the export statistics show that over 500 firms in the Chilean forest industries sector were exporting in the late 80s (compared with about 250 in 1983/84)[17] and as the seven largest firms' share of the sector's total export revenues fell from 80.5 per cent in 1986 to 63 per cent in 1990,[18] small and medium-sized firms had obviously emerged and stepped up their exports. It was unclear what led to the dynamic development of the many small and very small firms which are to be found in the various subsectors and previously supplied the generally undeveloped and still undemanding domestic market. The many new export firms indicate that the dualistic structure of the sector which dominated until the early 80s, with export-oriented large firms on the one hand and small firms geared to the domestic market on the other, had at least begun to change.

4   The Development of Competitive Advantages in the Wood-processing Industry as a Cumulative Learning Process

The competitiveness of the Chilean wood-processing industry has improved, if the agreed definition of international competitiveness is taken as a basis: the growing ability of a sector to export and rising national factor income are considered to be the most general indicators of the development of competitiveness. Market indicators (rising exports, product and market diversification, a positive trade balance, etc.) reveal whether the competitive position of a sector or economy has changed, but not how or why.[19] The following outlines learning and modernization processes at the level of enterprises and institutions with the object of shedding light on the dynamism of the development of competitive advantages in this world-market-oriented area of specialization. Particular attention is paid to the small and medium-sized enterprises (SMEs) that began exporting in the mid 80s.

Reorientation at Enterprise Level as the Transition is Made from Inward to Export Orientation

The crisis that occurred in the domestic market in the early 80s forced more and more SMEs to take a greater interest in exports. The growing number of export-oriented SMEs include sawmills, timber-processing firms (producing packaging materials, toys, wood for the interiors of buildings)

and furniture manufacturers. This trend saw an end both to the previously dominant export pessimism among SMEs and to the view circulated by the exporters of raw materials who had become established by the mid-80s that the Chilean wood-processing industry's competitive position would decline as soon as it distanced itself from the given comparative cost advantages (low wages, an unlimited supply of a cheap raw material).

The SMEs' growing export orientation was accompanied by a complex organizational and technological learning process. When they first changed their strategy, the "new exporters" had neither enough export know-how (transport, marketing, international quality standards, protectionism) nor sufficient manufacturing competence (knowledge of technology and the organization of work, management strategies, an adequately trained work-force). Consequently, many firms failed in their attempts to export. However, because of the inadequate business environment, even the successful firms needed a great deal of time and starting capital to find their way into the world economy and become accustomed to the production and commercialization techniques typically used at international level. They lacked the viable sectoral structures (e.g. efficient suppliers, systems that provide information on technological and market trends, technology-oriented institutions) on which enterprises in the industrialized countries can normally rely.

Exporting manufactures requires a high level of competence in all areas of business. The most serious problem the firms initially faced was recognizing the completely different requirements of the world market compared with those of the domestic market and translating them into appropriate corporate strategies. It was particularly important to improve such non-price aspects of competition as the organization of work, the technological level of production, product quality, design and image, the punctuality of deliveries and marketing. These heavy demands on the enterprises call for a specialization strategy and the use of external know-how (production- and export-related services). The SMEs, which remained inward-oriented until the mid-80s, were as a rule vertically integrated, had little contact with other firms/suppliers (autarchic mentality) and - because local demand was limited - offered a very wide range of products (from sawn timber through packaging materials to furniture). Overcoming these internationally uncompetitive entrepreneurial structures and strategies was not only a capital, know-how and technology problem but also a **mentality** problem: in the early stages of reorientation the first generation of "new exporters" were convinced of the efficiency and viability of the entrepreneurial concepts that had proved successful in the domestic market. Consequently, many initial attempts to export failed, and the continued application of past production concepts led to unwise investment.

Some furniture manufacturers, for example, report of visits to the USA to seek potential customers for their products. To appear as competent producers, they presented a very wide range of products of (as they see it today) mediocre quality. These first attempts failed, resulting at best in the potential customers visited asking for one or two samples. It is impossible to say how many firms fell at this hurdle. What can be said, on the other hand, is that some of the firms visited by our working group had already invested (unwisely) in new manufacturing equipment with a view to exporting a wide range of products and that some of this equipment was standing idle.

Stages in the Modernization of the Dynamic Enterprises

The enterprises made comparatively rapid progress in **marketing** and in acquiring and applying the necessary **export know-how** (quality standards, punctuality of deliveries, etc.). Both the large exporters of raw materials and the medium-sized firms have created **joint commercialization channels** (e.g. the establishment of a trading company, a joint marketing office set up by an employers' organization, trade associations), which ease the burden on individual firms in this field. This professionalization proved to be an important step in improving the competitiveness of the enterprises, which are hardly likely to find their way into the world economy acting alone.

It is evident from the technical problems (adaptation problems, incompetent maintenance, parts of the production apparatus at a standstill) encountered particularly - but not only - in technologically more complex branches of production (furniture, boards) that **manufacturing competence** and the technological level of production are still low. Integration into the world economy almost always coincides with the introduction of imported modern production equipment. That the introduction of production technologies commonly used elsewhere is no guarantee that their productivity and performance potential will be fully tapped is apparent, for example, from the board industry. Despite heavy investment in equipment, numerous technological adaptation problems are making it particularly difficult for this sector to achieve international quality standards.

The operating and maintenance personnel clearly do not yet have sufficient industrial manufacturing competence or technological know-how for the equipment (imported from the Federal Republic or Italy) to be used as it should be. A constraint encountered in some cases has been the inability of a firm's own engineers to repair technical faults on production lines (e.g. the failure of microelectronic control systems) and to solve fine-tuning problems in the linking of operations. Although experts flown in by the various machine manufacturers are able to correct technical faults quickly, the general problem of mastering the technology persists. Experience in industrialized countries shows that the installation and optimization of production lines based on the new production technologies is often a process of trial and error, in which close contact between makers and users is essential.[20] As a rule, the maker's and user's engineers work together to optimize production structures and processes. This cooperation does not end with the installation of the machines, but continues in order to ensure the continual optimization of production methods (incremental learning). These synergy effects, which stem from the close relationship between the makers and users of machinery, cannot be copied in Chile. Highly qualified engineers, on-going continuing training measures for production workers and technological and organizational cooperation among enterprises, which is lacking at present, is therefore all the more important.

Our observations confirm the findings of many empirical studies of technological change in Latin American enterprises, which have shown that firms must be capable of "imitative innovation" and independent "incremental technological change" if the productivity potential of modern production equipment is to be exploited.[21] The neoclassical conception of a given state of the art is a highly simplified view: "learning by doing" is not enough to ensure the successful application of technologies, their adaptation to the prevailing circumstances and constant incremental improvements to optimize production; active strategies and conscious decisions by management are also needed.[22] Unless money is invested in the training of workers and engineers, organizational changes are made and technological services are used to encourage technological learning in the firm, the efficiency potential of production equipment, however modern, will not be adequately tapped. As innovation in this sense of the term is a social process, it is one that can be shaped.

In Chile very few enterprises are currently making an active attempt to increase their manufacturing competence. The dominant view is that the introduction of modern machinery and **passive**, uncontrolled or unsystematic **learning by doing** will raise a firm to international productivity levels almost as a matter of course. This view is also reflected in generally inadequate investment in the **formation of human capital**. Although the dynamic exporting enterprises attach more importance to the training of their employees than the traditional, inward-oriented firms, the majority nonetheless consider unsystematic on-the-job training to be sufficient to ensure their workers attain an acceptable level of qualification. Training costs are often regarded as expenditure on consumption rather than an investment. Without wishing to belittle what the enterprises have done to modernize, it can be said that many entrepreneurs still see low labour costs as more relevant to competition than efforts to improve the organization of work or to increase productivity with training measures. This view is evident from the fact that only a few entrepreneurs are committed to the development of a training system in the wood-processing industry.

It is apparent that the competitiveness of firms is at present based solely on **partial rationalization efforts**. The conclusion drawn from an evaluation of the modernization process at enterprise level is therefore ambivalent:

- On the one hand, the sequence of modernization stages (marketing, introduction of new production equipment, limited efforts to improve technological competence, little training) reflects the requirements to be met when the transition is made from inward to world market orientation. Learning processes cannot occur simultaneously at all levels. The rapid improvement of marketing structures and the introduction of modern production equipment are likely to be of fundamental importance if integration into the world economy is to be at all possible.

- On the other hand, competitiveness will depend in the longer term on a constant increase in and the exploitation of technological and organizational potential at enterprise level. The tendency to prefer "soft-option" corporate strategies, which are still heavily based on the exploitation of the given factor endowment (low wages, enormous timber potential), was probably encouraged by the military dictatorship (through the suppression of trade unions, for example). There is a danger that this will prolong the "factor-driven phase" and slow the "investment-driven sequence", in which it will be essential to optimize existing competitive advantages and create new ones. The Chilean forest industries sector, in which these two development sequences currently overlap, should therefore heed Porter's warning of the drawbacks of this blocking mechanism during the transition from the export of natural resources to the export of manufactures: "In a narrow conception of international competition, competitive advantage results from factor abundance. ... In actual competition, however, the abundance or low cost of a factor leads to its inefficient deployment. ... Local abundance of basic factors lulls firms into complacency and deters the application of advanced technology."[23] All that needs to be added is that the application of modern technology must in turn be supported by changes in the organization of work and by training offensives.

Inter-company Relations and the Integration of Enterprises into Institutional Networks

In the early stages of world market orientation the new small and medium-sized exporters acted as individual, vertically integrated firms and did not try to cooperate with other firms or institutions. The absence of communication structures prevented rapid, joint learning processes and led these firms to take similar, costly misguided decisions (e.g. investment in equipment for the manufacture of too wide a product range). In recent years, however, approaches to "collective efficiency" structures[24] have gradually emerged. The modernization of inter-company relations and the formation of sectoral networks (vertical links and horizontal cooperation) are following the pattern at enterprise level (first, optimization of marketing, later - and still underdeveloped - cooperation in the technology and training spheres).

In the **marketing sphere** efficient private institutions or enterprises which were, interestingly, established or sponsored by the dynamic enterprises themselves have emerged. Marketing consortia, joint participation in trade fairs and marketing offices are improving competitiveness, particularly in the case of the SMEs.

Sectoral structures that might help to improve the **technological dimension** in the enterprises have hardly emerged so far. Instances of the enterprises themselves taking action in this respect are rare. They are often unaware that production-oriented services (e.g. maintenance, technical advice) or application-oriented research is vital if production efficiency is to be consolidated and increased. The absence of networks in the technological sphere leads to the dispersion of technical knowledge and hampers the rapid translation of technological know-how into improvements in productivity.

The Fundación Chile, a parastatal technology transfer agency,[25] is the only institution to have tried since the late 80s, with a high degree of success, to create an industrial technological environment and to give purposeful encouragement to technological learning processes in the (dynamic) enterprises by creating **communication and information structures** among the enterprises and between employers and experts (e.g. seminars on new production technologies, "round tables" for employers on technical and organizational problems at subsectoral level (furniture, boards, sawmills), continuing management training).

Besides undertaking these activities, the Fundación Chile is currently establishing in one of the major timber regions a furniture factory which will begin producing furniture parts some time in 1992. Although this firm is intended to operate profitably, it will also and above all perform an important **demonstration function**. As in very successful salmon-breeding and export projects run by the Fundación in the early 80s,[26] the aim is to show how best to establish and manage an enterprise in this sector that is capable of exporting: the production equipment at the furniture factory was installed under the guidance of international experts, and the workforce was trained at the factory's own centre, which will be made available to other interested parties in the future. In the first three years the firm will specialize entirely in the production of furniture parts in order to prepare the workforce for the manufacture of better-quality furniture. The enterprise invites potential new investors and furniture manufacturers to inspect the plant and will offer this target group seminars on technology, marketing and training.

The aim of the Fundación's project is to reduce serious constraints and to "form structures" (networks) in the wood-working industry:

- "Visual instruction" is used as a means of directly counteracting the lack of information and the traditionally individualistic attitudes of entrepreneurs.

- The training of workers, the importance of which is to be demonstrated at the factory, is to be professionalized and offered as a service to other firms.

- The installation of the latest production equipment, the emphasis on the organization of work and appropriate linking of work processes and the development of technological services (plant maintenance, repairs) will help to spread technological and organizational know-how.

The Fundación's involvement in the furniture sector will have an important catalytic effect on domestic and foreign investors and help to improve the regional location for the furniture industry.

If the still underdeveloped technological dimension is to be strengthened in the current process of structural change and if there is to be a lasting improvement in conditions for sustainable competitiveness, a major institutional effort will need to be made in the **training sphere**, where no serious attempts have yet been made to create a national training system.

"Islands of Efficiency" in the Wood-processing Industry as Stages on the Long Road to "Systemic Competitiveness"

To summarize these developments, advances in industrialization have so far been largely due to **modernization at enterprise level**. The wood-processing industry is thus still far removed from the model of "competitive industrial complexes" ("complejos integrados", "sistemas competitivos") that has been developed in imitation of the model adopted by the East Asian newly industrializing countries.

Although there are approaches to overcoming a sectoral structure that was highly dualistic until the mid-80s and signs of some "competitive structures" emerging, a sound business environment in the form of **"islands of efficiency"** exists for only a limited number of enterprises (most of which are already dynamic) and in only a few spheres (e.g. marketing).

It is becoming clear that the particularly successful enterprises abandon the incorrect vision of the vertically fully integrated firm and set their sights on a (vertical) division of labour and forms of (horizontal) inter-company cooperation. As a rule, these enterprises also develop contacts with sectoral institutions, universities and service organizations with a view to improving their external economies. In this way learning processes accumulate, communication structures emerge, the traditional distrust between firms is reduced, and **strategic groups of enterprises** form and purposefully shape their business environment. In this socio-economic process, which is dictated by market and competition and by cooperation that is not induced by the market (e.g. among enterprises or between enterprises and the Fundación Chile), the competitiveness of the dynamic enterprises and of the "strategic groups of enterprises" that have joined to form "islands of efficiency" is gradually improving.

These **network structures** will be illustrated with the help of three examples:

Formation of Structures Through the Establishment of Joint Marketing Enterprises

The marketing enterprise ASUN (Aserraderos Unidos) was established in the early 80s, acts as an export agency for some 25 medium-sized sawmills and manufacturing firms in the wood-processing sector and provides commercialization and export services. ASUN has a marketing office in Santiago, where it negotiates with buyers. It forges close links with customers, shares orders that are too large for the production potential of individual firms, handles its member firms' exports, gathers information on market trends and so helps to create **information and marketing channels** without which the SMEs could not gain access to international markets. These services enable the firms to concentrate on production.

Besides marketing, however, ASUN gives **advice on technology**. The enterprises that export through ASUN, some of which have been in existence for a long time, underestimate the requirements of the new markets when they make the transition to exporting. Despite the limited manufacturing complexity of their products (e.g. packaging materials, pallets), many enterprises found it almost impossible in the early 80s to guarantee uniformly high quality (e.g. timber sawn to the correct length, expert impregnation) and punctuality of deliveries. As the domestic market did not expect high quality, production equipment was not properly maintained, which led to losses of productivity and quality. ASUN's staff draw the manufacturers' attention to (often considerable) productivity potential that has not been tapped, maintenance techniques and necessary new investment, provide information on technological advances, carry out regular quality checks, which were not usual in the previously inward-oriented firms, and arrange meetings of all sawmill managers at irregular intervals for discussions of the normally similar technical and organizational problems the firms encounter. This division of labour has made rapid cumulative learning processes possible, accelerated and guided technological and entrepreneurial modernization efforts (the information provided by ASUN has at least reduced the incidence of misguided investment) and helped firms to acquire important export know-how (constant quality, flexibility, reliability and punctuality of deliveries). The result is a loosely networked group of competitive medium-sized sawmills with the marketing agency at its centre.

Forms of Horizontal Cooperation in Employers' Organizations

Another example is the employers' organization ASIMAD (Asociación de Industriales de la Madera), which was formed by medium-sized industrial enterprises in the wood-processing sector that felt poorly represented by the employers' association which is dominated by the large raw materials suppliers. Here again, the most important practical step in cooperation was the creation of joint marketing channels. The "ASIMAD enterprises" try to minimize the high transport costs and to offer a diversified range of products as a group. ASIMAD has an office in Santiago and acts as a central agency for importers to approach, establishes contacts between producers and buyers, organizes joint participation in trade fairs and is planning to open a showroom in Santiago so that the products of the furniture manufacturers in the south of the country may also be presented to potential buyers. Joint marketing has resulted in a more intensive exchange of information (on design, technical problems, etc.) among the enterprises, which has undoubtedly accelerated everyone's learning process. ASIMAD is seen in the wood-processing industry as an important information exchange for other enterprises wanting to export their products.

The Fundación Chile's Contributions to the Formation of "Competitive Cooperation Structures"

The various forms of cooperation among enterprises are complemented and reinforced by institutional networks. The "sectoral working parties" (mesas redondas) for "dynamic enterprises" (see above) initiated by the Fundación Chile has resulted in some enterprises exchanging engineers and inspecting each other's plants, which contrasts with their view in the past that they must isolate themselves completely from their competitors. These approaches could lead to the emergence of viable and dynamic **"competitive cooperation structures"**. The exchange of information among enterprises, the resulting increase in market transparency and the beginnings of networks of enterprises and institutions are

-   intensifying the competition (as enterprises attempt to emulate successful elements of other firms' strategies and to incorporate them in their own),

-   facilitating and accelerating individual and collective learning processes,

- creating scope for cooperation (e.g. in R&D, the specification of quality standards, the organization of joint seminars with the Fundación on technological problems),

- encouraging the identification of joint interests and

- enabling a sector that previously consisted of enterprises isolated from each other to become an entity.

The Fundación Chile is thus making major contributions to the formation of sectoral structures and proving how important institutions are in the process of developing competitiveness. So far, however, it has tended to be a welcome exception. On the whole, the existing institutions (e.g. small- and medium-scale industry promotion, training institutions) have been a less important group of actors in the process of industrial modernization than the dynamic enterprises. The institutions that played a vital role in the structural change of the 80s were (very largely) created by the dynamic enterprises themselves (e.g. ASIMAD). They are not therefore paving the way for structural change independently; their modernization and adjustment - inadequate thus far - to conditions and requirements changed by dynamic enterprises tends to come "after the event" (the exception being the Fundación Chile) - they are typical "latecomers".

Typical Development Pattern of the "Top Performers"

The observations outlined above indicate that the development pattern of the "best performers" among the dynamic enterprises as they make the transition from inward to world market orientation and try to become competitive is as follows:

- **Orientation towards international efficiency and quality criteria** raises the pressure of competition on the enterprises, mobilizes potential for creativity, creates potential for growth and triggers technological and organizational learning processes ("demand which provides the incentive to innovate"[27]).

- **Modernization at enterprise level** usually occurs in sequences: new technologies are introduced, commercialization problems are solved, the workforce then undergoes initial and advanced training, good technicians are trained, and work is organized.

- **Strategic groups of enterprises** form and establish horizontal cooperation structures and develop vertical links (e.g. ASIMAD,

ASUN), thus improving joint supply conditions and also (e.g. through imitation) increasing the internal pressure of competition (they develop "external advantages", "spread innovation throughout the economic structure"[28]).

- The enterprises or groups of enterprises form networks with **technologically innovative services**, institutions, universities (emergence of "systems of innovation"[29]). At this stage the whole group of enterprises becomes mutually supportive. Benefits flow forwards, backwards and horizontally. Or as Marshall says in his classical study on industrial districts: "The information flow is in the air."[30] Porter refers in this context to "clusters of industries".[31]

This development pattern (which also suggests a time dimension) conforms to Carlota Perez's analysis of the development of competitiveness:

"The new standards of competitiveness do not favor isolated enterprises, but those that can profit from the synergy of strong creative networks. They do not favor static enterprises, but those that can constantly innovate." The networking of enterprises and the interplay of enterprises and institutions lead to the emergence of a "national system of innovation". The formation of highly competitive structures is based on "network building, consensus building, focusing on results, decentralization, continuous learning, continuous improvement ... and, obviously, competition as an 'ally' in restructuring."[32]

As these modernization sequences have hitherto been confined to "islands of efficiency", the "catch-up modernization" of the far from efficient business environment is essential if the sector is to develop sustainable industrial competitiveness and consolidate its world-market-oriented specialization. In the future all concerned will need to make even greater efforts to establish in the wood-processing industry a highly competitive "technico-social system"[33] that is capable of learning and feedback.

Networks[34] of enterprises and of enterprises and institutions are appropriate in this context both at the pre-competition stage (e.g. cooperation between several enterprises and universities in basic research, cooperation between government and enterprises on the specification of standards) and at the competition stage (e.g. technological cooperation among enterprises, joint marketing).[35] Network structures as an alternative to the highly vertically integrated enterprise that tries to subcontract as few activities as possible are particularly appropriate

- where complementary factors of production can be supplemented and combined, thus enabling costs to be reduced (e.g. the exchange of important know-how on markets and technology, the exchange of engineers, joint commercialization: additions to product ranges);
- in sectors where R&D costs are particularly high and "resource pooling" therefore becomes interesting;
- in sectors where rapid changes in demand and economic instability make heavy investment by the individual enterprise to establish a secure competitive position a very hazardous undertaking and risk-sharing therefore makes better sense than it does in growth segments. [36]

Many studies show that, as such network structures and joint learning processes call for fair contracts between the partners and good personal contacts (confidence), they exceed what is otherwise usual in market relations among entities engaged in economic activities. [37]

Policies restricted to the macro level are obviously not enough to ensure the comprehensive modernization of the national location and the emergence of an industrial/technological environment. On the other hand, dynamic development in the Chilean wood-processing industry also shows that a stable, outward-oriented macro policy is in itself capable of mobilizing considerable potential in enterprises for creativity, growth and modernization.

5   The Importance of Old and New Export Enterprises

The "Model and Catalytic Function" of Small and Medium-sized Exporters

The structural change that has occurred since the mid-80s has led to the emergence of a growing number of small and medium- sized enterprises, which are now competitive. They paved the way for a second export phase, which began with the export of processed wood products. Until the late 80s the large enterprises in the sector concentrated on the export of primary goods and sawn timber and made little attempt to industrialize. The efforts made by the large enterprises to modernize should not be underestimated, however: for one thing, they have now attained an international level in primary goods and sawn timber; for another, the new investment some enterprises are now beginning to make and their plans for industrial projects indicate that they are likely to be responsible for the bulk of investment in the processing of timber in the future.

The new small and medium-sized exporters (with export earnings from about US $ 300,000 to US $ 7 million) are of secondary importance when viewed in purely quantitative terms (contribution to foreign exchange revenues, etc.). Nonetheless, they have shown that

- even SMEs are capable of integrating into the world economy and of doing so
- with exports of manufactures, which not even the large enterprises had previously succeeded in doing.

This trend has multiplier effects:

- In recent years the SMEs have modernized their plants extensively, penetrated markets and accumulated export know-how, without being able to make large profits during this start-up phase. Past learning processes and investments are only now beginning to translate into economically visible results.

- Both existing enterprises and new investors are being guided by the successes of the pioneering exporters (imitation effect) and overcoming their fear of international competition. The large enterprises are being joined by a rapidly modernizing "SME substructure".

- Although a sound sectoral environment has yet to emerge, the enterprises that are modernizing and the new investors can now take advantage of the experience (partly institutionalized in ASIMAD and ASUN, for example) of the "pioneering exporters". This is facilitating and accelerating learning processes.

- Not even the investment decisions of the large enterprises are likely to be completely unaffected by the success of the SMEs in industrialization. Cracks can now be seen in the still widespread dogma that the further the Chilean forest industries sector removes itself from static cost advantages (cheap timber, low wages), the less competitive it will become.

Despite this, the SME scene is far from idyllic: export enterprises that are now small by international standards must grow to an internationally typical size in the future.

The New Type of Entrepreneur

Growing world market orientation has helped to produce a broader stratum of businessmen and a "new type of entrepreneur". Unlike their counterparts in other Latin American countries, Chilean entrepreneurs (including those in the SME sector) have overcome their fear of international competition and made considerable progress in such areas as management, quality requirements, marketing and punctuality of deliveries. Nonetheless, the "new entrepreneurs" are not yet (on the whole) advocates of an integral, comprehensive modernization project. Their priorities do not include investment in human capital, the modernization of labour-management relations or technological innovation. Chile does not have the industrial and craft traditions and inclinations that characterize the European or even the East Asian enterprise culture.

The dynamic Chilean entrepreneurs have so far been particularly neglectful of the primacy of technology, technological competence and the organization of work as determinants of sustainable competitiveness and of the fundamental importance of the productivity of labour as an indicator of economic efficiency. They often focus their attention less on changes in their enterprises and the development of existing and new products than on "the market", the trend in exchange rates and price fluctuations in their market segment. They are thus more interested in safeguarding existing competitive advantages than in creating new ones (reactive rather than active behaviour). They have accepted the world market as a frame of reference, but continue to take a very static view of competitiveness ("We do what the market requires").

It is not surprising in these circumstances that, while viable marketing structures have emerged, entrepreneurs have made little effort to join forces with a view to improving the technological infrastructure and the training system. Studies of international competitiveness refer to the relevance of entrepreneurial attitudes towards product development and especially of technical progressiveness as major determinants in the development of competitive advantages.[38] Chile still has some catching up to do in this respect.

6   The Relationship between Entrepreneurs (or Their Organizations) and Trade Unions in the Context of Democratization and World Market Orientation - the Socio-political Dimension of Competitiveness

The competitiveness of the forest industries sector is not, in the final analysis, determined solely at sectoral level: economic development is always a politico-social process.

The Basic Political Consensus

A marked feeling of distrust between entrepreneurs and trade unions, the entrepreneurs' reservations about (democratic) government and the fear of great social pressure from the trade unions for distribution - after almost two decades of military dictatorship - seemed to impose serious restrictions on the environment for the formulation of an economic policy acceptable to society after the coalition of Christian Democrats and Socialists took power in March 1990. As the change was made from authoritarian to democratic government, it was widely feared that - given the backlog of social demands from the lower and middle classes - the consolidation of economic development might be neglected for a time at least. Our surveys of the forest industries sector and its environment qualify the validity of these scenarios. There is a political consensus between the government alliance, "Concertación", the employers' associations and the trade unions that

- Chile's economic development will continue to be based on world market orientation;

- a sustainably viable social policy is not simply a question of redistribution (zero sum game): it must be compatible with the country's economic development;

- the return to democracy is important in itself and must be defended whatever economic and social crises may occur.

This basic consensus underlies the reorientation of those involved in the process of democratization and gives the Economics Ministry more freedom to pursue active strategies aimed at improving the competitiveness of the economy, with the participation of all concerned.

The Trade Unions

Not least because they are aware of the catastrophic situation in other Latin American countries, the trade unions have accepted that there can be no going back to the conditions of the 60s and the inward-oriented model. They support the goals of world market orientation and an improvement in the country's competitiveness and are prepared to join productivity alliances in which the object is both to ensure a high rate of investment and to increase the scope for real wage increases and pursue an active social policy to alleviate absolute poverty. Union activities are, moreover, no longer focused solely on wage rises, as they were in the 60s, but increasingly on job security, health policy, training opportunities, pollution at the work-place, etc. and thus, in more general terms, on improved working and living conditions and also the overdue modernization of enterprises in these areas. The unions are likely to have been prompted to change their attitude partly by the higher wages the more up-to-date exporting enterprises are normally able to pay (because of increases in productivity) and the better working conditions they offer compared with the traditional, undynamic inward-oriented enterprises. It must be borne in mind that after almost twenty years of military dictatorship the development of trade unions capable of taking action and asserting their interests against the well organized enterprises is a medium-term project.

The Entrepreneurs (and Their Organizations)

The entrepreneurs (and their organizations) are aware that they must come to terms with democracy, that a return to authoritarian government is very unlikely and that they have no alternative but to accept the democratic parties and the trade unions. They do not therefore represent an active opposition to the government, even though they were very much in favour of Pinochet staying in power before the referendum on the continuation or termination of the dictatorship. Most of the "new entrepreneurs" have no fixed political home, but they are guided by the philosophy of the Chicago school. The fixed point in their ideologically influenced thinking is "the market", which they consider as responsible for resource allocation as for industrial relations, solving the problems in the education and health sectors and even preventing environmental degradation. The "new entrepreneurs" see themselves as the protagonists of economic change, a task which tended to be assigned to government until the mid-70s (where it also belonged according to the entrepreneurs of the time). The new entrepreneurs feel completely independent of government and regard themselves as being at least equal negotiating partners.

Orientation towards the world market has undoubtedly led to the "modernization of entrepreneurial awareness" both economically and in terms of culture and policy. Compared with their counterparts in other Latin American countries, Chilean entrepreneurs now have a far less pronounced subsidy- and rent-seeking mentality, and not even SMEs are afraid of international competition. Most are also well aware from their business trips, visits to trade fairs and inspections of plants in western democratic countries that they derived considerable profit margins from Chilean "capitalismo salvaje" and the accompanying authoritarian suppression of trade unions and democratic parties. This awareness may be at the root of the marked pragmatism and realism that characterizes the attempts being made by the employers' associations to define their place in democratic society. The divergent views of different employers' associations and individual entrepreneurs on the trade union question, collective bargaining and the right to work and strike show that there is as yet no definite commitment to a model of industrial relations which the employers take as their guide. Considerable interest is therefore being shown in experience in various democratic countries.

Clearly, the employers' associations too are actively trying to redefine their role in society. After two years of the new government and an initial period of deep suspicion of "Concertación" (a Socialist as Economics Minister was seen by most entrepreneurs as a distinct threat) enterprises are now more willing to talk to the administration and trade unions.

Social Cooperation

To summarize the attitudes and changes of view of the social actors and their search for orderly means of settling conflicts within the framework of a growing basic consensus, it can be said that all concerned are showing a considerable degree of flexibility and willingness to compromise. The existence of the basic consensus that has been outlined and the acceptance of fundamental social rules do not mean that political, social and economic conflicts will no longer occur in the future. The participants have, however, agreed on the new contours of a **socio-economic corridor** in which future conflicts will be settled. All sections of society are thus pursuing a common aim, which will enable their potential for creativity to be pooled and forces to be combined, strengthen the national capacity for transformation and support the administration's ability to establish policies and strategies.

Seen through Western European eyes, this meeting of the minds on the foundations of the development of society seems banal, but it is significant when Chile is compared with other Latin American countries, where this basic consensus has yet to emerge. It encourages the formulation of a longer-term development strategy geared to macroeconomic needs and the expansion of the social, political and ecological dimension of the world-market-oriented development model. In Chile there is thus the prospect of the development of a vision of future change, whereas other countries of Latin America tend to be characterized by manifestations of social decay, political polarization and a paralysed apparatus of state.

7   Conclusions

> *"Competitive advantage is created and sustained through a highly localized process. Differences in national economic structures, values, cultures, institutions, and histories contribute profoundly to competitive success. The role of the home nation seems to be as strong or stronger than ever. While globalization of competition might appear to make the nation less important, instead it seems to make it more so. ... The home nation takes on growing significance because it is the source of the skill and technology that underpin competitive advantages."* (M. Porter, The Competitive Advantage of Nations, New York 1990, p. 19)

It became clear that making the transition from the "easy phase of export orientation" to the goal of "competition-oriented industrialization" and developing competitive advantages is not a linear, quasi-automatic process, but depends on lengthy - though optimizable - entrepreneurial and social processes of searching and learning, institution-building and the emergence of national technological competence. The Chilean wood-processing **industry** is still at the beginning of this process. In view of the profound structural change that has occurred since the mid-80s, however, there is room for optimism. The continuation of the export-oriented growth strategy is based on stable, transparent macro policies and "clear rules of the game" for those who engage in economic activities. Policies relating specifically to the wood-processing industry (meso level) are also needed to help it overcome its structural problems (see box).

Structural policies to improve systemic competitiveness in the Chilean forest industries sector

-    **Training:** The level of training of many workers, especially in small and medium-sized enterprises, is low. As the existing inter-company training centres have been neglected in recent years, they are no match for the new requirements. The development of a modern training system is urgently needed if the sector is to press ahead with technological and organizational modernization. This calls for close cooperation between government, enterprises and trade unions.

-    **Technology:** Small and medium-sized producers in particular lack such production-related services as the drying and impregnation of timber and maintenance, repair, planning and installation services for equipment and machinery. These shortcomings could be overcome by installing technical service and information centres in the wood-processing regions to provide such services and to advise entrepreneurs on technical and organizational matters.

-    **Information networks:** Few enterprises have sufficient knowledge of export markets and recent technological advances. The creation of open information structures is therefore essential. An agency assisted with public funds, but run by employers' associations, might, for example, collect, file and computerize information on markets, prices, environmental protection standards and new trends in the international timber markets by carefully studying the relevant international press and the universally accessible electronic sources of information and make it available to interested enterprises as a service. The flexible forms of cooperation among successful small enterprises in the "third Italy" might be taken as a model for this.[40]

-    **Promotion of the establishment of small and medium-sized enterprises:** The entry into the market of new, young enterprises in sectors where value added is higher is important for the dynamism of the sector's industrialization. New SMEs, however, often have difficulty obtaining venture capital for the start-up phase, during which they can expect to have little or no revenue. They are likely to make profits only when they have become established in the market. Private banks prefer to become involved with young enterprises only when the start-up phase has been completed, whereafter their value can be expected to rise sharply. The Economics Ministry might set up guarantee funds to minimize the difficulties initially encountered by promising SMEs. Other approaches to promoting innovative SMEs would be tax concessions for enterprises spending on R&D or undertaking industrial research with other enterprises at the pre-competition stage.

-    **Protection of resources:** Ecologically irresponsible overuse of forests and land must be prevented and the preservation of the several million hectares of the Chilean rainforest, the only one in the moderate southern latitudes, ensured by legislation on protection and use. The democratic government is in the process of amending the Forestry Act to this end. Contrary to short-sighted views, ecologically sustainable use of the natural forest together with the creation of nature conservancy areas and the expansion of environmentally less harmful plantation agriculture would be a major competitive factor for the Chilean wood-working industry in view of the growing international awareness of the environment. This would require clear legislation and effective supervisory institutions and instruments.

It will be appreciated that there is a need to strengthen a sectoral environment in which the enterprises compete, but also complement each other and cooperate at the pre-competition stage (cooperative competition) in order to create a sectoral **structure** which is efficient and capable of learning and adapting (systemic competitiveness). We thus agree with the conclusion drawn by Schmitz from his analysis of processes of SME modernization that "the issue is not whether small enterprises have growth and employment potential but under what conditions."[39] Views differ on the importance to be attached to the various determinants of modernization. Schmitz's analyses suggest that "collective efficiency" is essential for the successful modernization of SMEs and that modernization at enterprise level can be virtually derived from it.

Our study suggests that the development of competitive factors very much depends on the ability of enterprises to modernize, for which institutional or inter-company networks are no substitute. It is the already dynamic enterprises which are capable **not only** of increasing their own efficiency but also of tapping further potential for rationalization in an inter-company division of labour and through institutional networking. "Collective efficiency" thus occurs only if there is **potential for modernization** in the enterprises. As a rule, undynamic enterprises are not only overextended by internal requirements but also able to take little advantage of external offers and development potential (e.g. R&D funds, complementary opportunities for specialization).

This means that government or public institutions cannot **create** competitive structures, this essentially being a task for the enterprises themselves. But public institutions can and certainly must make a crucial contribution to promoting the **modernization potential** of enterprises and backing technological and organizational innovation and learning processes with appropriate policies.[41] Chesnais is therefore right when he says: "Government assistance in the strengthening of forms of co-ordination and co-operation previously identified by enterprises, notably small and medium enterprises, may lead to a development of externalities on which competitiveness can build and an expansion of the total 'system' within which industrial and technological learning processes take place."[42]

The concept of "systemic/structural competitiveness" is first and foremost a model that is opposed to simplistic market ideologies. However, this view also implies a criticism of excessively etatist planning approaches. In Chile as elsewhere the impending modernization of the economy cannot be a state-technocratic act. Unlike classical **Keynesianism**, which concentrated primarily on **demand-oriented macro policies**, the emphasis in the structural policies needed to improve the industrial location and the **supply conditions** of enterprises is on decentralized decision-making structures. In the industrialized countries industrial policy is pursued more at regional and local level than at national level. Experience in industrialized countries (e.g. the Federal Republic of Germany) shows that regional industrial policy is no longer based solely (or is based less and less) on the classical means of intervention, i.e. legislation (trade policy and import bans, for example) and money (subsidies, promotional funds), but is complemented by such consensus-oriented "soft guidance instruments"[43] as the flow of information, conviction, pooling the know-how of various actors, integration of interests and the adoption of procedures.

The growing importance of "soft guidance instruments", the increasing relevance of efficient channels of communication between major social groups, institutions and organizations is revealed by the "regional conferences" that have formed in some Länder of the Federal Republic, especially in crisis-hit areas where comprehensive restructuring is about to begin (e.g. North Rhine-Westphalia).[44] Government acts as a broker, "facilitating the blending of abilities and promoting structural networking".[45] Many of those involved are trying to agree on future development prospects, to identify bottlenecks in the process of modernization, to anticipate (ecological and social) modernization costs with a view to reducing them and so to establish guidelines for political and entrepreneurial decisions. Socio-economic networks embracing employers' organizations, trade unions, associations, local administration, institutes of technology and universities are emerging in the regions. They occupy a position between government and market (meso level), elaborate visions - or, put more pragmatically, scenarios - of regional development, prepare strategic decisions of principle and make non-etatist political control of economic restructuring programmes and the active and anticipatory shaping of structures possible.

Why such control of market processes is necessary is explained by Hillebrand:

"Countries which fail to develop a strategic perspective as the guide for corporate and government action and largely rely on spontaneous, ad hoc reactions and processes of trial and error underestimate in particular

- the importance of the timely and resolute development of physical and above all non-physical infrastructure for the international competitiveness of enterprises,
- the time it takes to develop the main determinants of international competitiveness, human capital and technological infrastructure, and
- the adverse effects which uncertainty and risks have on aggressive corporate strategies".[46]

These new approaches to industrial and technology policy differ significantly from "hierarchical, excessively etatist control concepts" and require social actors who are efficient and capable of compromising, learning and transformation. In Chile this process of institution-building and the **active shaping of structures** to improve the economy's "systemic competitiveness" is still very much in its infancy. The direction to be taken, however, has been mapped out: "Although it sounds like some bureaucratic council with a lot of institutes, a successful national system of innovation is more a set of behaviour patterns harmonizing public and private organizations towards a common national goal. It involves deliberate consensus building to define a development strategy and move towards it; as well as deliberate construction of appropriate institutions to promote innovations and steer structural change and to systematically increase structural competitiveness."[47]

Notes

1 See, for example, **CEPAL,** Changing Production Patterns with Social Equity, Santiago de Chile 1990; **CEPAL,** Equidad y Transformación Productiva: Un enfoque Integrado, Santiago de Chile 1992.

2 For an explanation see **D. Messner / J. Meyer-Stamer,** Lateinamerika. Von dem "verlorenen Jahrzehnt" zur "Dekade der Hoffnung"?, in: Blätter für deutsche und internationale Politik, No. 1, 1992.

3 **S. Lall,** Building Industrial Competitiveness, OECD, Paris 1990, p. 11.

4 The article is based on the findings of an empirical study undertaken in Chile in the spring of 1991 by a German Development Institute working group. The empirical phase consisted largely of interviews with 55 enterprises (average duration, including an inspection of the plant: about 4 hours) and discussions with experts in all the various institutions with close links to the forest industries sector. The author was joined in the study by Ingolf Dietrich, Jürgen Friederici, Roland Guttack, Kerstin Kiehl und Wolfram Klein. See **D. Messner / I. Dietrich / J. Friederici / R. Guttack / K. Kiehl / W. Klein,** Weltmarktorientierung und Aufbau von Wettbewerbsfaktoren in Chile - Das Beispiel der Holzwirtschaft, GDI, Berlin 1991 (also available in Spanish).

5 See **O. Muñoz,** Crisis y reorganización industrial en Chile, in: Notas Técnicas, No. 123, Santiago 1988, pp. 9 f.; **P. Meller,** Revisión del proceso de ajuste chileno de la década del 80, in: colección estudios CIEPLAN, No. 30, 1990.

6 **L. Mármora / D. Messner,** Chile im lateinamerikanischen Kontext - Ein Modell für Demokratisierung und Entwicklung in der gesamten Region?, in: D. Nolte (ed.), Modellfall Chile?, Hamburg 1991.

7 **F. Chesnais,** Science, Technology and Competitiveness, in: OECD (ed.), Science, Technology, Industry Review, No. 1, 1986, p. 86. A similar view is taken in other, more recent studies on competitiveness, although they differ widely in the importance they attach to the various factors and in the conclusions for economic policy they then draw. See, for example, CEPAL, 1990, op. cit.; **M. Porter,** The Competitive Advantage of Nations, New York 1990; **M.H. Best,** The New Competition, Cambridge 1990; **W. Hillebrand,** Industrielle und technologische Anschlußstrategien in teilindustrialisierten Ländern, GDI, Berlin 1991; in Development of a Competitive Strategy: A Challenge to the Countries of Latin America in the 90s, GDI, Berlin 1991, K. Esser outlines the challenges that outward orientation poses for the Latin American countries and attempts to distinguish sequences in the development of competitiveness.

8 The diagram emerged from the author's discussions at the German Development Institute with his colleagues Wolfgang Hillebrand und Jörg Meyer-Stamer.

9 See, for example, **M. Dauderstädt,** Free Markets versus Political Consensus - The International Competitiveness of Societies, in: Intereconomics, January/February 1987; also: **M. Olson,** The Rise and Decline of Nations, New Haven and London 1982.

10 The approach should not be seen as functionalist. A state-technocratic strategy to make the various influencing factors compatible with the goal of "producing competitiveness" ("blueprints") would be hopelessly overextended. It is important to grasp the societal and social dimension of "competitiveness" (and of socio-economic development as such) in order to correct the reductionism of mainstream economics. Experience shows that quite different development styles and forms of regulation can contribute to the emergence of viable economies. "Workable markets" are undoubtedly only one element of the "wealth of nations", which is likely to depend primarily on the mobilization of creativity in society. Just as wrong as the "functionalist version" of this concept, of course, would be the assumption that absolutely any approach is viable.

11 "Forest industries sector" is used in the following as a synonym for "sector forestal", the standard term in Chile. The sector is divided into the forestry sector (forest management) and the wood-processing industry, which is appropriate since this is the classification used in the Chilean literature and statistics.

12   Timber production rose by 87 per cent from 1974-80 and by a further 42 per cent from
      1980-87, the furniture industry growing initially by 120 per cent and, from 1980, by
      37 per cent. Timber exports increased from US $ 9 million in 1970 to US $ 152 million
      in 1987. Paper and cellulose exports rose from US $ 33 million to US $ 365 million in
      the same period.

13   For further details on the ecological problem see **D. Messner et al.**, Weltmarktorien-
      tierung ..., op. cit., pp. 31-39 and 130-132.

14   **World Bank,** Chile: Forest Industries Sub-sector Study, Washington, August 1986.

15   Investment has risen sharply, especially since the late 80s. To give but a few examples of
      the considerable sums involved: in 1991 a new cellulose plant (Arauco II) of the Celulosa
      Arauco y Constitución company went on stream at Concepción (amount invested: about
      US $ 500 million); in the mid-90s a cellulose unit is due to start production at the "For-
      estal Valdivia" plant (amount invested: about US $ 1200 million); the Japanese company
      Daio Paper is planning to set up a sawmill, a cellulose unit and a woodchip plant near
      Valdivia (amount to be invested: about US $ 600 million); the Tierra del Fuego company
      is planning to construct a sawmill, a cellulose plant, a woodchip plant and an export
      terminal in the Xth region (amount to be invested: US $ 290 million); the CAP company
      is planning to construct a fibreboard plant in der VIIIth region; the Chilena de Fosforos
      company is constructing a plant for the manufacture of chopsticks; the French company
      Philippe de la Roche is planning to manufacture hardwood windows and doors, etc.

16   According to **INFOR,** Estadisticas forestales 1989, Santiago 1990.

17   **R. Aldunate,** El mundo en Chile, Santiago 1990, p. 176.

18   See **INFOR,** Exportaciones forestales chilenas, Santiago, March 1991, p. 3, and **R.
      Contreras,** Más allá del bosque, Concepción 1988, p. 248.

19   **H.-D. Feser,** Technologische Wettbewerbsfähigkeit und internationaler Handel, in: idem
      (ed.), Technologische Entwicklung und internationale Wettbewerbsfähigkeit, Regensburg
      1990, p. 23.

20   For the furniture industry see **V. Döhl et al.**, Neue Rationalisierungsstrategien in der
      Möbelindustrie, Munich 1989.

21   For an overview see **B. Herbert-Copley,** Technical Change in Latin American
      Manufacturing Firms: Review and Synthesis, in: World Development, No. 11, 1990.

22   See **M. Bell,** "Learning" and the Accumulation of Industrial Technological Capacity in
      Developing Countries, in: M. Fransman / K. King (eds.), Technological Capability in the
      Third World, London 1984; **J. Katz,** Technological Innovations and Comparative
      Advantages ..., in: M. Fransman / K. King (eds.), Technological Capability in the Third
      World, London 1984; **J. Meyer-Stamer et al.**, Comprehensive Modernization on the
      Shop-Floor: A Case-Study of the Brazilian Machinery Industry, GDI, Berlin 1991.

23   **M. Porter,** op. cit, pp. 82 f.

24   This term was coined principally by **H. Schmitz,** who similarly emphasizes the impor-
      tance of efficient structures and networks in his studies of the development of small
      enterprises in developing countries. See, for example, **H. Schmitz,** Flexible Specialisa-
      tion in Third World Industries, IDS, Sussex 1990.

25   For the Fundación Chile see **F. Meissner,** Technology Transfer in the Third World - The
      Case of the Chile Foundation, New York 1988.

26   See **T. Huss,** Transfer of Technology: The Case of the Chile Foundation, CEPAL
      Review, No. 43, 1991, pp. 110 ff.

27   **F. Chesnais,** op. cit., p. 111.

28   **F. Chesnais,** op. cit., pp. 111/120.

29   See **C. Perez,** The Institutional Implications of the Present Wave of Technical Change
      for Developing Countries, discussion paper for a World Bank conference on "Long-Term
      Economic Growth Prospects", Washington, November 1988, p. 27. Perez considers the

establishment of "national systems of innovation" to be of prime importance if there is to be a sustainable improvement in the competitiveness of economies.

30   **A. Marshall,** Principles of Economics, London 1920.

31   **M. Porter,** op. cit., p. 151.

32   **C. Perez,** op. cit., p. 27.

33   **K. Esser,** Anmerkungen zur wirtschaftlichen und politischen Transition in Lateinamerika, in: D. Nolte (ed.), Lateinamerika im Umbruch?, p. 44.

34   The term is cogently expounded by **W.W. Powell** (Neither Markets nor Hierarchy: Network Forms of Organisation, in: Research in Organizational Behaviour, Vol. 12, 1990, p. 13): "... in network modes of resource allocation, transaction occurs neither through discrete exchanges nor by administrative fiat, but through networks of individuals or institutions engaged in reciprocal, preferential, mutually supportive actions. Networks can be complex: they involve neither the explicit criteria of the markets, nor the well organized routines of the hierarchy. A basic assumption of network relationships is that the parties are mutually dependent upon resources controlled by another, and that there are gains to be had by the pooling of resources. In network forms of resource allocation, individual units exist not by themselves, but in relation to other units. These relationships take considerable efforts to establish and sustain, thus they constrain both partners' ability to adapt to changing circumstances. ... Complementarity and accommodation are the corner-stones of successful production networks."

35   See **F. Chesnais,** Technical Co-operation Agreements between Firms, STI-Review, No. 4, OECD, 1988; **D.J. Teece,** Towards an Economic Theory of the Multiproduct Firm, in: Journal of Economic Behaviour and Organization, Vol. 3, 1982.

36   See, for example, **G. Dosi,** Sources, Procedures and Microeconomic Effects of Innovation, in: Journal of Economic Literature, Vol. 26, September 1988.

37   See, for example, **W.W. Powell,** op. cit.

38   See, for example, **H.-D. Feser,** op. cit., p. 30; **B.B. Schlegelmilch,** Der Zusammenhang zwischen Innovationsneigung und Exportleistung, Ergebnisse einer empirischen Untersuchung in der deutschen Maschinenbauindustrie, in: Zeitschrift für betriebswirtschaftliche Forschung, No. 40, 1988.

39   **H. Schmitz,** op. cit., p. 13.

40   See **F. Pyke et al.,** Industrial Districts and Interfirm Co-operation in Italy, Geneva 1990.

41   For further details see **D. Messner et al.,** Weltmarktorientierung ..., op. cit., pp. 125-142.

42   **F. Chesnais,** op. cit., p. 120.

43   **W. Krumbein,** Industriepolitik: Die Chance einer Integration von Wirtschafts- und Gesellschaftspolitik, in: U. Jürgens / W. Krumbein, Industriepolitische Strategien, Bundesländer im Vergleich, Berlin 1991, p. 40; also: **A. Klönne et al.,** Institutionen regionaler Technikförderung, Opladen 1991.

44   See the papers in **U. Jürgens / W. Krumbein,** Industriepolitische Strategien, Bundesländer im Vergleich, Berlin 1991.

45   **J.E. Aubert,** What Evolution for Science and Technology Policies?, in: OECD Observer, February/March 1992, p. 5. Aubert similarly emphasizes the role of government as broker in the technology policy sphere.

46   **W. Hillebrand,** op. cit., p. 185.

47   **C. Perez,** op. cit., p. 27.

Comprehensive Modernization on the Shop-Floor: A Case Study on the Machinery Industry in Brazil

Jörg Meyer-Stamer

1   Introduction

Terms of Reference

After decades of import-substituting industrialization Brazil today possesses a complete set of industries. Brazilian enterprises are capable of producing virtually everything, though mainly at a relatively high price and with a somewhat dubious quality.[1] International competitiveness is relatively low, and manufactured exports rely to a large extent on state subsidies. Now facing grave financial problems, however, the state can no longer sustain a policy of subsidization. Unfortunately, only few enterprises can today meet international efficiency standards since in Brazil's inflationary environment, raising prices has always been a much easier option than raising productivity. Furthermore, after ten years of investment being deterred by a turbulent economic environment, the technological gap between Brazil and advanced countries is widening.

The maxim *business as usual* therefore cannot be a realistic option for Brazilian entrepreneurs and policymakers. The National Development Bank (BNDES) was the first to react to this problem. Traditionally one of the agents of a development policy which tried to reduce dependency, three years ago BNDES set about promoting Brazil's competition-oriented integration into the world market. This, the bank argues, should be based on internationally competitive private enterprises capable of investing in R&D, of producing efficiently and of cooperating with foreign enterprises.[2]

The new government which took office in March 1990 shares this view. It pursues a gradual opening of the Brazilian economy to international competition. The new policymakers consider the stagnation of Brazilian industry as being all the more grave in view of the radical changes taking place in industry at the international level. The old, Fordist model of industrial development via automation and intensive division of labour, which laid the foundations for the economic and social progress in the developed countries, is running out of steam. In the industrialized countries, industry's initial reaction was to intensify the old model, i.e. introduce computerized flexible machinery and try to govern the production process using information and communication systems. This, however, did not reverse the general trend of declining productivity growth.[3] After a phase of costly learning, enterprises reoriented their strategies. They began to understand the necessity of *comprehensive modernization* on the shop floor, i.e. linkage and articulation between *technical, organizational* and *social* innovations. It seems that this is essential for meeting drastically changing market requirements calling increasingly for *quality, flexibility* (i.e. the ability to produce very differen-tiated products) and *responsiveness* (i.e. the ability to react very fast to changes and differentiation in customer behaviour).[4]

Enterprises wanting to compete on the world market can therefore most probably no longer rely on a Taylorist rationalization strategy, one which delivers efficiency but an insufficient level of quality, flexibility and respon-siveness. This means that Brazilian enterprises are facing a new challenge. Some of them have been exporting for quite some time to compensate fluc-tuations on the domestic market. The others will now have to face interna-tional competition as a result of recent changes in industrial policy, particu-larly regarding market access.

Comprehensive Modernization: The Brazilian Experience So Far

The industrialization regime of the past put virtually no pressure on compa-nies to operate to international standards of efficiency, and the economic and political instability of the past few years provided no incentive for introducing any profound changes. Moreover, given the state of industrial relations (which are paternalistic and at the same time highly conflictive) and the existence of a "capitalist class that has not gone through the civi-lizing experience of confronting and negotiating with its class adversary",[5] implementing cooperative management concepts is an undertaking which can be expected to be fraught with difficulties in Brazil.

What Brazilian scholars currently report[6] is a profound change in the *organisational structure* of industrial enterprises, with quality circles and new logistics concepts in particular having been introduced on a broad scale. The diffusion of *technical* innovations is less advanced; for instance, there are very few CNC machine tools or robots.[7] Finally, *social* innovations are very rare, a fact which may be somewhat surprising in view of the presence in Brazil of several international automobile manufacturers. In the industrialized countries these companies rank among the pioneers of three-dimensional concepts of innovation.[8] In Brazil they pursue a partial innovation strategy of "computer-aided Taylorism" plus partial Japanisation: technico-organisational innovations without relaxing the division of labour, without broadening skill recommendations, and without transferring responsibility to the shop floor.[9] Even just-in-time systems are only being implemented between enterprises, not within. JIT between enterprises implies merely shifting stocks towards the suppliers, and Brazil cannot thus secure the rationalisation effect which industrialized countries have achieved by restructuring their entire logistics chain. Even the stabilizing effect of long-term supplier contracts is absent since such contracts have so far not been observed in Brazil.[10]

For enterprises in industrialized countries, quality and responsiveness vis-à-vis a volatile demand structure are as important motives for modernisation as cost considerations in the narrower sense of the term. Most Brazilian enterprises have few problems with the former two factors as it is not very difficult to sell high-price/low-quality products on the domestic market. They accordingly show a low propensity for R&D spending, a preference for short-term planning, resistance to joint undertakings to strengthen their technological base, and a tendency towards imitation and dependent behaviour.[11]

There are three further reasons for the only sluggish spread of new manufacturing technologies:[12]

- in an environment of low labour costs, automation is often economically not viable,

- the costs of automation technology are high,

- the general economic crisis has cut back the level of productive investments.

Nevertheless, radical technical change has recently invaded some parts of Brazilian industry, especially those producing for the external market.

"... the great motivating factor for modernisation and automation is competitiveness in the international arena. In the most advanced firms, the target is to at least remain close to the global best practice system. It is the international market which sets the standards by which the managers structure their decision-making processes"[13]

A strategy which aims to introduce not only technico-organisational innovations but also "post-Taylorist" industrial relations can work in Brazil, as can be seen from the experience of some companies in the metalworking industry.[14] In the early eighties (a time of grave economic crisis), the machinery firm Semco, for example, eliminated most levels of its hierarchy and switched to a system of self-regulated work teams. By so doing it succeeded in enhancing its productivity and competitiveness, even against competitors abroad.[15]

However, there can be no doubt that enterprises like Semco are exceptions. Enterprises producing for the domestic market prefer to practise business as usual. Technico-organisational-social change is thus accentuating the polarisation within Brazilian industry, with some internationally competitive best-practice enterprises at the one extreme and the majority of traditional enterprises viable only under a market protection regime at the other. Here, the ideas and structures inherited from import substitution represent a barrier to innovation.

The following example demonstrates some consequences of maintaining inherited organisational structures:

"In a production site of a metallurgy enterprise producing precision products and materials the very latest and expensive CNC machine tools were being introduced. The workers were not allowed to alter the programs developed by the programming department. However, they did so (without the management knowing this) in order to maintain a continuous production process. At the same time they demanded formal training in programming. This being rejected the workers one day decided not to correct the mistakes they discovered in the programs (what exactly accorded with the rules). The result was a paralysation of production in the following steps of production since the produced parts did not fit the norm although everything had been conducted according to the established rules."[16]

This example raises two issues. Firstly, it seems that the potential of Taylorism is overestimated and the scope for shop-floor-oriented schemes of organisation underestimated. Secondly (and most importantly), it is the explicit interest of the management which forms the basis for applying computer-aided Taylorism. "Managements want workers to follow orders, not improve the production process."[17]

Workers and their trade unions do not necessarily oppose the introduction of new manufacturing technologies; on the contrary, they demand that such innovations be accompanied by a modernization of industrial relations (which in Brazil signifies guaranteed bargaining autonomy, for example), and an upgrading of the skill level of the workforce.[18]

Structural Features of Brazil's Machinery Industry

The production of non-electrical machinery (NEM) contributes 2.7 per cent to the GNP (1987), and it has a 9 per cent share in total manufacturing value added, which makes the machinery sector Brazil's third largest industrial sector (after the chemicals and food processing industries).

Three events stimulated the build-up of a machinery industry in Brazil:

-   The worldwide recession of the early thirties compelled Brazil - like other countries - to start substituting goods it had previously imported. National entrepreneurs (often of Italian origin) founded capital goods companies in that period.

-   The opening of the country for foreign direct investment in the fifties attracted a number of international companies; in some cases they were encouraged to invest in Brazil by multinational companies producing consumer durables who found it difficult to import the equipment they needed.

-   After the first oil price shock, intensified import-substituting policies led to an expansion of domestic demand, and the source of growth shifted from private domestic demand to public demand. National as well as multinational companies set up operations in the capital goods industry.

In 1979, after the second oil price shock, public investment fell back and left the machinery sector with excess production capacity. The sector suffered a severe setback. The capital goods on demand segment reached its lowest level of production in 1984, when output was only 72 per cent of the 1979 record figure. Serially produced goods slumped to their lowest in 1983 at only 53 per cent of the 1980 output figure.[19] The sector hardly recovered in the mid-eighties. Total output of non-serial capital goods amounted to only 50 per cent of the 1980 output figure.[20]

During the recession of the early eighties, employment was slower to contract than production. Nevertheless, the machine tools subsector was affected severely by cutbacks in public and private investments. Exports reached only three quarters of the 1980 figure in 1982, the number of machines sold that year was only 5 per cent of the 1980 figure, and employment plunged to its lowest level in 1983 at 48 per cent of its 1980 level.[21]

Employment and output advanced slowly after the mid-eighties until this process came to an abrupt end when the new government took office in March 1990. For more than one year, Brazil faced extremely turbulent economic and political conditions, and the present situation of the machinery sector is therefore precarious:

-   In the first quarter of 1991 its production fell by 70 per cent compared with the same period one year previously.[22]

-   The sector has experienced radical cutbacks in employment in recent months. Whereas lay-offs affected 44,000 workers in 1990, 20,000 workers were laid off in January and February of this year alone.[23]

-   In some companies 70 per cent of installed capacity is already idle.

The present situation of industrial enterprises has been determined largely by two events: the overall recession and the end of import substitution policies. While producers of machine tools and special machinery are generally suffering under the impact of the recession, the heavy equipment subsector is more severely affected by the drop in domestic demand. This subsector's major problem is its strong dependence on public investments, as its enterprises have been producing mainly for large-scale government projects, e.g. power plants, ports, installations in the steel or petrochemical industry.[24] Public investments, already low in 1989, fell by a further 44.5 per cent in 1990.[25] One large heavy equipment firm reported not having received a single order over the past year. The financial situation of many enterprises has been aggravated by the state's habit of delaying payments.[26]

While opening up the market will have only a slight immediate influence on the heavy equipment subsector, the machine tools and special machinery subsector will be profoundly affected by the arrival of international competitors. With planned average import tariffs of 20 per cent,[27] it will be quite easy to import technology and machinery of superior quality from international suppliers.

Today three main bottlenecks appear to jeopardize the future of Brazil's machinery sector: product technology, marketing channels, and production efficiency. Successfully handling the following challenges will therefore be of fundamental importance to the future of the sector:

It will have to upgrade its *product technology*. Compared to other NICs, Brazil is lagging behind technologically in this sector. One appropriate measure would be a significant increase in in-house R&D expenditure. The legislation on information technology should be amended to create a more flexible frameowkr for importing microelectronic equipment.

Faced with periods of low or at least highly fluctuating domestic demand, the sector will have to look for new *export marketing channels* to avoid becoming paralyzed.

The lack of national technological upgrading has caused the gap between Brazil and its international competitors to also widen in terms of *process technology*. There is only little evidence of computerized equipment and new forms of production organization.

Research Design

The non-electrical machinery sector (NEM) has never been a prime candidate for Taylorist rationalization strategies: small batch sizes were not compatible with transfer-line-based mass production, and the workforce has always had a comparatively high skill profile. This, however, did not prevent Brazilian enterprises from implementing Taylorist schemes, trying to augment the division of labour as far as possible in order to achieve the greatest possible control over the workers and the labour process. Comprehensive modernization, thus, is without any doubt an issue for this industry. In fact, it is a much more urgent issue here than in other industries which are currently mass-producing (e.g. automobile, electronics, household appliances and others). In our view, because of inherent sectoral characteristics and changes in international best practice, the Brazilian machinery industry is a very probable candidate for comprehensive modernization. This is even more likely since the regulatory environment for Brazilian industry is changing dramatically. For the sector, modernization is a question of do or die.

Based on the available literature, what we expected to find was

- an only moderate diffusion of new manufacturing technologies, i.e. CNC machine tools, flexible manufacturing cells/systems and CAX-technologies (CAD, CAE, CAQ); however, we expected the diffusion level to be higher in foreign than in national enterprises;

- relatively strong evidence of organizational innovation, i.e. cellular manufacturing using traditional machinery, new logistics concepts and total quality control;

- very little evidence of social innovation, i.e. devolution of responsibility to the shop floor (e.g. shop-floor programming), job-enrichment, a less pronounced division of labour, and teamwork.

The main questions were:

- Is a strategy of comprehensive innovation viable in the Brazilian environment?

- Can Brazilian enterprises become more competitive via a partial strategy, i.e. a focus on organizational modernization with only limited technical and social innovation?

- Is the skill level of the workforce sufficiently high to make a less pronounced division of labour viable?

- Are organizational and social innovations viable in an environment of notoriously conflictive industrial relations?

- Are there systematic differences between national and foreign companies?

To select the enterprises for the field study sample we applied four criteria:

- a reasonable mix of serial and non-serial producers;

- a mix of national and foreign companies;

- a focus on medium and larger enterprises since these present better preconditions (e.g. professional management) for handling comprehensive modernization;

-    a mix of enterprises from different regions.

We selected 23 enterprises - five national and nine foreign machinery enterprises (machine tools and special machinery enterprises), and five national
and four foreign equipment enterprises (see Table 1 in the annex). Our
sample covered eight of the ten biggest enterprises in each sector in terms of
turnover.[28]

2   Results of the Field Survey: Technical Innovations

Computer-Aided Automation Technologies in the Production Process

The main technical innovations in the production area are CNC or DNC
facilities, flexible manufacturing cells or systems and other "CAx" elements
(CAD or CAQ). In our sample, eleven of the 23 firms (48 per cent) had not
introduced any of these technical innovations. Of these eleven firms, nine
belong to the equipment industry, two to the machinery industry, five are
foreign, and six are national. Five firms had introduced CNC technology
without other elements of computer-aided automation. All belong to the
machinery industry, two are national and three are foreign. Six firms use
CNC technology together with "CAx"-elements. Two of these are equipment industry firms, four are machinery industry firms, three are national,
and three are foreign. In this group we found the only two firms which had
implemented flexible manufacturing cells (one is a national machinery
industry firm, the other a foreign equipment industry firm).

Of the 23 firms in our sample, eight had introduced a CAD system. No
significant differences were found regarding nationality or type of industry.
With the exception of one case, however, the CAD systems were used only
for limited tasks, e.g. special parts families or the design of electronic
boards. We found only three firms which had networked CAD and CAM.
Two of these are national, one is foreign, and all are machinery industry
firms. Obviously due to the high investment costs, no company had yet
introduced a flexible manufacturing system.

Concerning for the motives for technical modernization, it is no surprise in
the current period of economic recession that "raising productivity" and
"improving economic performance" are regarded as the most important
motives. We did not expect, however, the high rating given to improving

product quality. It can be assumed that there exists a certain backlog demand for precision machinery.

Reduction of lead-time is an important motive, especially for firms using advanced technology. All firms which have introduced just-in-time systems give a rating to reducing lead-time. This demonstrates the relevance of this factor in improving the production process. On the other hand it is surprising that two firms in the equipment industry see no necessity whatsoever to reduce lead-time by modernization; all other equipment industry firms give this factor a high rating. Views in the equipment industry on the importance of reducing lead-time clearly differ.

"Raising flexibility" and "improving innovation capability", which are advanced as decisive advantages of computer-aided automation in literature, are not identified as important motives for modernization by the majority of the firms in our sample. It is interesting to note, however, that the technologically advanced firms rate these two motives significantly higher than the firms which have not introduced computer-aided technology. This may be a sign of the latter's unawareness of the advantages of computer-aided automation. Obviously, flexibility and capability to innovate have not so far been important factors of competitiveness on the national market.

Regarding the factors which obstruct technical innovation, the fact that the "general sales situation" is rated highly again shows the impact of the recession on corporate decision-making processes.

The factors "availability of equity" and "access to bank credits" are each given very different ratings which reflect the breakdown into foreign and national firms. For most of the foreign firms, availability of equity and credits is not a problem at all because of their financial linkage with the parent company. For national firms, however, technical modernization seems to be closely associated with financial problems.

A surprising result - particularly in view of the legislation on information technology - was the very low significance attached to "access to technology" as an obstructing factor. The firms in our sample reported having few problems in obtaining the type of technology they wanted. A glance at the circumstances of the various types of firms explains this result. The foreign firms have no problems in obtaining technology because of their connections with their parent companies which in some cases made it possible for them to circumvent the prohibitions of the information technology legislation. On the other hand, as most of the national firms which give a low rating to "access to technology" factor had not yet introduced computer-aided technology, it is not surprising that they are content with sourcing their technology from the national market. The few national firms which produce with relatively advanced technologies are somewhat more critical of the restricted access to technology, though without giving it a high rating as an obstacle to modernization.

On the matter of the compatibility of hardware and software, the answers from national and foreign firms differ significantly. The foreign firms have more problems probably because they use both national and foreign hardware and software.

The Diffusion of Computerized Material Resources Planning Systems

A material resources planning (MRP) system is usually introduced to

- enhance the transparency of the production process,
- reduce lead-time and throughput time,
- reduce stocks and work in progress.

In our research we found ten enterprises which operate computer systems with a degree of integration sufficiently high to presume the existence of truly computerized MRP; the degree of integration turned out to be the central criterion here since some enterprises designated their simple computerized stock administration systems as MRP systems. The other 13 enterprises included only one case of a failed attempt to introduce MRP, the failure here having been due to resistance from certain levels of management within this foreign company. Although failed MRP ventures are a rather familiar experience in industrialized countries, our survey did not identify such failures in any other companies (at least none admitted having had an experience of this type).

The group of ten MRP users comprised six national and four foreign enterprises, five machinery manufacturers and five equipment manufacturers. This distribution is surprising insofar as the non-MRP enterprises all agreed that the introduction of MRP made no sense for them because of the peculiarities of their products and production processes. Our findings do not support the view that MRP systems are unsuitable for companies manufacturing highly complex, highly customized products.

The main motives for introducing MRP were, not surprisingly, the wish to reduce delivery-response and throughput times, slash production costs, reduce stocks and improve capacity utilization. Enhancing proximity to the customer was seen as a minor motive. However, some differences did emerge between national and foreign companies. National companies rated reducing throughput time, reducing stocks and greater proximity to the customer significantly higher than foreign companies. It seems that national companies are more strongly committed to new logistics concepts.

Unanimously, the enterprises saw the investment costs as the major obstacle to introducing an MRP system. Other factors were of relatively minor importance, though the responses differed clearly on the role of the lack of MRP vendors and lack of model enterprises. The divergence here can be explained by examining the dates when the enterprises launched started their MRP projects: early beginners suffered more from the lack of vendors than the latecomers. Regarding the lack of model enterprises, foreign companies attach less importance to this point than national companies as many of them have access to systems developed by/for their respective parent companies. However, even they differed considerably in their answers here, and even more so in those concerning the role of MRP vendors. Non-users attached less importance to all these points; presumably they are not aware of the problems linked to the introduction of MRP.

Four enterprises with well-developed MRP systems, only one of them foreign, reported that the introduction of the MRP system had been accompanied by changes in the division of labour and the materials flow within the enterprise. Two others reported changes in the division of labour, and two further companies had flanked the introduction of MRP with organizational changes to achieve internal JIT.[29] A reasonable degree of reorganization had thus been undertaken to make the MRP system viable. However, reorganizing the factory did not necessarily imply decentralization: six enterprises integrated operational data collection into their system, indicating an intention to use the system for centralized monitoring, and only one enterprise reported systematically using the knowledge available on the shop floor.

On the other hand, nine enterprises reported having kept their informal information channels open. Although this seems to be inconsistent with the above statements, it is not necessarily a contradiction and can be interpreted as a tendency towards centralization and decentralization simultaneously: the management knows (or at least should know) that the factory simply will not operate with rigid planning regime but nevertheless wants to maintain the *potential* to control any process at any time.

3 Results of the Field Survey: Organizational Innovations

Internal Just-in-Time (JIT)

Internal JIT is by no means widespread. Only five enterprises in our sample, all of them national companies, have introduced internal JiT. All have implemented cellular manufacturing, and two of them also reported additional innovations to rationalize the material flow.

Findings in the Machinery Sector

Identifying families of parts is generally considered to be the first step in implementing cellular manufacturing. Because batch sizes are larger in the machinery industry than in the equipment industry, we expected that machinery manufacturers would have fewer difficulties in standardizing their production and would therefore be in a better position for introducing cellular manufacturing. In fact, this was one of the main reasons for distinguishing between machinery enterprises (which we expected to be engaged more in serial production) and equipment enterprises (which tend to have much smaller batch sizes).

Surprisingly, only two of the 14 machinery enterprises had realized internal JIT, this after previously introducing cellular manufacturing. One of the two enterprises is still at an initial stage, manufacturing only standardized products representing an insignificant fraction of total production in the cell. The other enterprise with a relatively new concept of cellular manufacturing presents a different picture. Although internal JIT here is still in the initial, experimental phase (introduced in late 1990), this enterprise has been able to reduce its throughput time from eight to three weeks and at the same time make considerable reductions in the number of staff on the shop floor.

Both enterprises introduced teamwork within the cell. Workers in the team are expected to operate all the machines there, which initially meant that they had to undergo additional training. Additionally, responsibility for quality control was transferred to the cell team. Although a certain degree of control and supervision still exists, comparison with the pre-cell situation shows a relaxation in the division of labour.

A third enterprise operated with teamwork in the assembly area, where machines were assembled by a team and its foreman with the shop-floor workers being responsible for coordinating the assembly work.

The three points most frequently mentioned as an incentive to introduce JIT were reduction of stocks, improvement of order response, i.e. lead-time, and reduction of transition time.

As these objectives were mentioned unanimously, the question remains why only two of the enterprises have actively begun to implement JIT innovations. A more detailed examination of the obstructing factors reveals that macroeconomic problems are the main obstacles. Four companies considered the inflationary environment to be the decisive factor holding back JIT. The general demand situation was also considered to be an important factor, though this is a problem which has no directly obstructive impact. Obviously, fear of inflation is seen as the predominant reason hindering the introduction of JIT.

The enterprises which did not use JIT techniques pointed out two further arguments which appeared to us to be the main "subjective" factors. Six companies stated that for their enterprise JIT was not necessary; two companies argued that JIT was not feasible (figure 1).

These six enterprises emphasized that reducing throughput time has traditionally been one of their major concerns. They seemed to be fully satisfied with their performance and did not intend to further investigate into matter,

Figure 1: Companies' Positions On Internal Just-in-Time					
	Not feasible	Not necessary	Technol. approach	JIT implemented	Special cases
Machinery industry	2	6	1 MRP 1 FMS	2	2
Equipment industry	3	2	-	3	1

largely, it seems, because their main customers are not demanding shorter lead-times. When asked about their perception of JIT, it turned out that their main concern was to deliver on time. This is generally accomplished by "working harder" when the time schedule is tight, an approach which apparently does not allow for systems solutions. The fact that two enterprises from the same subsector and with a comparable product range have successfully implemented JIT could cast some doubt on the validity of these statements.

As there is only one enterprise which has amply introduced JIT and a second which has implemented the rudiments of JIT, a search for common characteristics does not make much sense. Nevertheless, there is one conspicuous similarity: these two companies are among the largest in the sector.

Findings in the Equipment Sector

In the equipment industry the question of internal JIT was a highly controversial issue. Most enterprises in our sample stated that their batch size of one and highly complex production process made a JIT system non-viable (figure 1).

By contrast, three enterprises stressed that the high complexity of the production process is a major incentive for implementing JIT. As lead-times in this sector are generally long, the potential for reducing them is considerable. These enterprises did not agree that the high number of items involved represents a major constraint to identifying families of parts.

In our sample of nine enterprises, three national enterprises operate with a considerable internal JIT component. Not surprisingly, their most important motives for introducing internal JIT were reduction of stocks, changes in the turnover of stocks, and reduction of lead- and transition times. The most important obstructing factor was resistance from middle management, though opinions on this factor were not unanimous. The second obstructing factor was the vast organizational restructuring generally considered to be necessary when introducing JIT.

The references to these two problems signify that some enterprises in this sample have realized that introducing JIT is not predominantly a technical problem but requires an analysis of the organization of the production/assembly process. In many cases, this results in the dismissal of staff at middle management level.

The Organization of Quality

Due to the policies of import substitution and market protection, most markets in Brazil have an oligopolistic structure. Quality has therefore been a secondary issue until recently. The consumers of final and intermediate products had no alternative but to live with low quality standards. An international consultancy found that an average of 25,700 out of every million parts produced in Brazil are defective, compared to only 200 on the international market.[30] As the opening of the market - a central element of the Collor government's industrial policy - will make quality an important determinant of competitiveness on the local market, Brazilian enterprises will increasingly have to address themselves to this issue.

Available evidence indicates that quality problems of Brazilian industry have two sources: an underdeveloped quality control/assurance system within companies and an inadequate supply structure. Both are important factors within the framework of a comprehensive modernization strategy. Companies in the industrialized countries have started changing their internal quality organization.

One of the central elements of comprehensive modernization is the integration of hitherto distinct and separate parts of the production process, including product quality control which with the conventional "exclusive format" was carried out as a separate operation. In the new strategy, quality is no longer controlled downstream but is assured by the shop-floor staff during the production process. The aim is "not to control quality, but to produce quality".

On the other hand, quality presupposes a high standard of technical equipment in the form of high-tech precision machines (e.g. CNC machines) and high-tech control equipment to measure quality.

We tried to classify the enterprises interviewed into the following three strategy categories:

- Technology - assuring quality by using high-tech equipment, in most cases high-tech control equipment;

- Separation - maintaining or enlarging of "external" quality control stations;

- Integration - transferring responsibility for quality to the shop-floor staff.

Since only one enterprise is pursuing a purely technology-based strategy and one other is pursuing a separation strategy, these two categories must be neglected here. A strategy of integration had been favoured by seven enterprises.

The technology strategy and the integration strategy are not mutually exclusive since nearly one half of the enterprises pursue a joint strategy of technology and integration, indicating a tendency towards comprehensive modernization in this area. The figures also indicate that national machinery companies are more interested than foreign companies in improving quality by pursuing a strategy of integration and technology (four out of five national enterprises follow this strategy, compared with only two out of nine foreign enterprises). Of course, one could argue here that the national industry is under greater pressure to improve its quality.

The enquiries regarding strategy also concerned quantifications in terms of quality improvement. Although ten enterprises are following a strategy of technology and integration and even 17 enterprises have at least integrated quality control into the production process, only two enterprises could quantify the resulting improvements in quality. Both are national enterprises manufacturing capital goods (equipment industry). One enterprise reported reducing quality costs from 5 per cent to 1.4 per cent of its net profit. The other reported a reduction in waste of about 60 per cent between 1987 and 1990.

The poor response to this question suggests that although all enterprises regard quality as very important, only very few address themselves to this issue systematically.

Of the 17 enterprises intending to pursue a strategy of integration and technology or at least integration, only 6 have so far also made changes to their organizational structure, defined as changes in the corporate hierarchy or a reduction or relocation of quality control personnel. The changes concerned were a shift centralized to decentralized quality control stations and the reduction or relocation of quality inspectors, in one case from 107 to 47.

4   Summary of Findings

Two main conclusions emerge to summarize our findings:

-    A strategy of comprehensive modernization is viable in the Brazilian machinery industry and probably in Brazilian industry as a whole.
-    There are no clear-cut factors which explain why certain companies have opted to pursue this strategy.

Some of our findings did not verify our expectations. For instance, in terms of the spread of *new manufacturing technology* we found no systematic difference between national and foreign companies; nor was there any identifiable correlation between high exports and the introduction of modern technologies. The degree of differentiation within both the foreign and the national group was striking: in each we found both CIM-oriented enterprises and companies with a very low level of technical sophistication. In the former group, the introduction of technology has not implied a tendency towards deskilling; on the contrary, the opposite seems to be the case. It can therefore be concluded that there is no tendency towards "computerized Taylorism", i.e. substituting skilled workers by "intelligent" machinery. Considering the import restrictions it is somewhat surprising that companies do not consider access to technology to be a major obstacle. Not at all surprising, however, is the fact that national enterprises emphasize their limited equity capital and limited access to credits as being major obstacles to modernization.

Nor is there any systematic difference between national and foreign companies in terms of their utilization of *MRP*. In most cases the introduction of MRP has been accompanied by the extensive organizational restructuring which is a prerequisite for its efficiency. It seems that enterprises here are pursuing a strategy of "centralized decentralization" which tries to make detailed data available centrally while at the same time leaving a reasonable level of autonomy on the shop floor.

In terms of *organizational innovation*, we found only four cases of large-scale restructuring at shop-floor level, mainly in the form of introducing cellular manufacturing. Remarkably, all these cases were national enterprises (four out of ten), and three of them were in the equipment industry (three out of five).

There seems to be no general strategy to raise *quality* standards by the extensive use of computerized machinery. In this respect, firms tend instead to combine two approaches: introducing new testing and measuring equipment and integrating production and quality-assuring operations.

Summarizing these findings, we can distinguish four types of enterprise (see table 1 in the annex).

- Companies without explicit modernization strategies: six cases, evenly distributed between the national and foreign, machinery and equipment categories.

- Companies with technology-oriented modernization strategies, where a distinction can be made between three types: seven are enterprises with a modest level of technical modernization, i.e. in most cases some CNC technology, most of them foreign machinery enterprises. Four are enterprises with a medium level of technical modernization, i.e. CNC plus CAD or MRP. Two enterprises have a high level of technical modernization, having implemented all three types of system and aiming to implement CIM.

- Companies focusing on organizational and social innovations: only one national machinery enterprise is pursuing this strategy.

- Companies with truly comprehensive modernization strategies: three national equipment enterprises have opted for this path.

These findings were not in line with our expectations. The level of technical modernization is somewhat higher than expected, that of organizational modernization somewhat lower. We would not say, though, that any enterprise in our sample is showing a tendency to repeat the industrialized countries' experience of "technical overkill". Even the scale of technical innovation is at best reasonable; in many cases it is very poor. Indeed, there are many reasons for not rushing to introduce new manufacturing technologies in Brazil, e.g. the very high price of the equipment and the very low price of labour. It therefore makes sense that we did not encounter any cases of flexible manufacturing systems or automated transport devices and only very few cases of flexible manufacturing cells and machining centers. Nevertheless, many company representatives held the view that certain parts can only be machined with CNC machines for reasons of quality, and productivity (NC/CNC machinery operates at much higher speed) and quality were indeed found to be the main motives for introducing this type of equipment. Quite a number of companies therefore face the challenge not only of introducing organizational and social innovations but also of investing heavily in manufacturing technology.

Contrary to our expectations, it hardly makes sense in our sample to differentiate between organizational and social innovations since in three out of four cases organizational innovations in the logistics area were associated with basic social innovations. It is noteworthy that all enterprises with organizational and social innovations are located in the hinterland of Sâo Paulo; we found no such case in the city of Sâo Paulo or its ABCD-region (i.e. the southern industrial suburbs). It seems that because of a history of highly conflictive industrial relations in Sâo Paulo and the ABCD-region, neither capital nor labour is capable of imagining social innovations. Indeed, such innovations would have to be based on a sound basis of trust which certainly does not exist today. Although most companies reported a very low level of employee fluctuation and many reported having trustful relations with their workforces, the trust concerned is of the paternalistic type. We encountered only one enterprise (located in the interior) with a works council, with a more modern approach to regulating industrial relations.

However, we cannot argue that industrial relations are more "modern" in the interior of Sâo Paulo state or in other federal states than in metropolitan Sâo Paulo or its ABCD area. Paternalistic structures are present everywhere, even in companies where social innovations have been introduced. Unlike in industrialized countries, in Brazil it was not the workers fighting for participation who achieved these innovations.[31] On the contrary, they were imposed on the workers in a voluntarist way by a paternalistic management aware of modern management techniques. We discovered only top-down strategies and not a single case of interactive, participative planning of the restructuring of shop-floor operations. Brazilian enterprises thus have at best a limited view of social innovations. They make use of the worker's knowledge in day-to-day operations but not in planning the production process.

To some extent these facts can be explained by the position of the trade unions, whose main concern is the struggle for wage increases to counteract the downward wage trends of the past years. Another important issue is the struggle for power between different national federations of trade unions, a struggle which is being fuelled by the federal government which is trying to weaken CUT, the largest federation. Furthermore, particularly within CUT, socialist and reformist factions are still fighting about the general line of trade union policy. The preconditions for drawing up active trade union strategy on modernization are simply not fulfilled in Brazil.

We found no reason to believe that the skill level of the workforce is a major obstacle to comprehensive modernization. The main obstacle is in fact the unstable, unpredictable economic environment which deters investments and thus slows down the modernization process. Most companies seem to operate as if their market were to remain closed because they mistrust the government's policy. They perceive the government more as a generator of turbulence than as an institution capable of bringing about a restructuring of production. This is particularly true of foreign enterprises. Although we found only very few companies which were considering closing down their Brazilian operations, foreign companies are generally somewhat more sceptical than national companies about the overall economic situation.

This hesitant, defensive posture of foreign companies may partly explain the fact that there is no "social technology transfer" within multinational enterprises in this sector. Probably Brazilian subsidiaries are learning to accept the importance of social and organizational innovations, but they certainly lag several years behind their parent companies in this respect. Indeed, contradicting international and to some extent even Brazilian experience, quite a number of foreign companies were not in the least inclined to acknowledge the viability of such innovations in their industry.

In the case of most foreign and many national companies, it seems that structural conservatism, unawareness of the benefits of new organizational concepts, and scepticism regarding their viability are major reasons for the relative absence of organizational and social innovations. Another factor is that as competitive pressure is low, enhancing flexibility and responsiveness are not presently matters of strong interest to machinery firms in Brazil. Beyond this, an industrial company obviously cannot handle all problems at once, and to many companies in Brazil it may seem that coping with erratic demand, fluctuating inflation, and profound and frequent changes in exchange rate, trade and industrial policies is more important than introducing innovations on the shop floor.

Figure A-1: Data on the Sample Companies

Company	Ownership	Location	Turnover (Mio. US-$) 1990	1989	Average export ratio(%)	Employees Most recent	before lay-offs	Products	Modernization strategy
Machinery Industry									
A	National	Interior S.Paulo	100	115	14	2300	3300	Machine tools	High technology
B	National	Interior S.Paulo		52	40	1100	2000	Machine tools	Organizational/Social
C	National	ABCD		11	0	200	800	Machine tools	no
D	National	Municipial S.Paulo	25		5	450		Machine tools	Medium technology
E	National	Rio de Janeiro	30	50	7	780	2400	Valves, drillers	Medium technology
F	German	Interior S.Paulo	20		20	160		Machine tools	Modest technology
G	German	Municipial S.Paulo	40	60	25	450	600	Spec. mach. for automotive industry / refrig. product.	Modest technology
H	Dutch	Paraná	10	30	30	380	500	Machine tools	Medium technology
I	German	Municipial S.Paulo	n.a.		10	540	825	Machine tools	High technology
J	German	ABCD	50		30	240	320	Machines to squirt plastic materials	Modest technology
K	German	ABCD	60	62	50	1100	1300	Presses, cylinders, rolls	Modest technology
L	German	Rio Grande d.S.	38	39	30	346	357	Cotton cleaning machinery	no
M	Japanese	Municipial S.Paulo			0	46		Machine tools	no
N	German	Interior S.Paulo	8	8	10	85	160	Machine tools (assembly only)	Modest technology
Equipment Industry									
O	National	Interior S.Paulo	60	n.a.		1200		Locomotives, turbines, equipment for mining etc.	Comprehensive
P	National	Interior S.Paulo	12	22	10	250	350	Turbines, compressors	Comprehensive
Q	National	Interior S.Paulo	102	102	3	2800		Sugar & alcohol; steel mills; cement, mining; castings	Comprehensive
R	National	Interior S.Paulo	90		10	1600	3500	Sugar & alcohol; equipm. for ports & mining, turbines	no
S	National	Municipial S.Paulo	40	98	10	1100		Turbines; equipment for ports & mining	Medium technology
T	German	Municipial S.Paulo	270		22	4679		Paper machines, turbines and pumps etc.	no
U	German	Municipial S.Paulo	35	small		370	500	Painting equipment for car industry	Modest technology
V	French	Interior S.Paulo	50		50	740	3500	Turbines; irrigation- and petrol industry equipm.	no
X	German	Interior S.Paulo		7		173	230	Service; reducers & gears	

Remarks: ABCD = Industrial agglomeration south of São Paulo (Santo André, São Bernardo, São Caetano, Diadema)

Notes

1   See **C. Frischtak,** Industrial Regulatory Policy and Investment Incentives in Brazil, World Bank (mimeo) 1989; **J.H. Sequeira,** World-Class Manufacturing in Brazil. A Study of Competitive Position. São Paulo: American Chamber of Commerce Publications Division, 1990, and the results of a recent Brazilian industry survey presented in "Diagnóstico do atraso", Veja, 27 de Fevereiro 1991.

2   **BNDES,** Strategic Plan 1988/90, Rio de Janeiro 1988.

3   **G. Bell,** Technical Change and the Productivity Paradox, OECD Observer, No. 164, 1990.

4   See for instance **H. Rush / J. Bessant,** The Diffusion of Manufacturing Technology, OECD Observer, No. 166, 1990; **K.H. Ebel,** Manning the Unmanned Factory. International Labour Review, Vol. 128, No. 5, 1989, pp. 535-51; **G. Vickery,** Advanced manufacturing technology and the organization of work. STI Review, No. 6., 1989. The same issue is being adressed in the current discussion on "lean production" ; see **J.P. Womack et al.,** The Machine that Changed the World, New York: Rawson, 1990.

5   **G. O'Donnell,** Challenges to Democratization in Brazil. World Policy Journal, Vol. 5, No. 2, 1988, pp. 281-300.

6   See **A.G. Alves Filho et al.,** Fordism and New Best Practice: Some Issues on the Transition in Brazil. IDS Bulletin, Vol. 20, No. 4, pp. 7-13, 1989; **J.C. Ferraz et al.,** Tajetórias de crescimento e a modernização da indústria brasileira: Um cenário para a década de 90. Rio de Janeiro: Universidade Federal, Instituto de Economia Industrial, 1990; **A. Fleury,** The impacts of microelectronics on employment and income in the Brazilian metal-engineering industry, Genf: ILO (Technology and employment programme), 1988; **A. Fleury / M. Salerno,** Condicionantes e Indutores de Modernização Industrial. Texto preparado para o seminário internacional "Padrões Tecnológicos e Processo de Trabalho: Comparações Internacionais" São Paulo (mimeo), 1989; **M. Leite,** O trabalhador e a máquina na indústria metal-mecânica. São Paulo: LABOR Instituto Eder Sader, 1989; **R.R. Lima,** Implementing the "Just in Time" Production System in the Brazilian Car Component Industry. IDS Bulletin, Vol. 20, No. 4, 1989, pp. 14-17; **J.A. Neto,** Automação industrial e seus impactos econômicos e organizacionais no setor mecanicos: bens de capital. In DIEESE (ed.), Para um Levantamento Sistemático dos Impactos Socio-Econômicos da Automação Microelectrônica, São Paulo (mimeo), 1988; **A.J.C. Prado,** A difusão da automação microeletrônica na indústria de autopeças brasileira e seus impactos socio-economicos. In DIEESE (ed.), Para um Levantamento Sistemático dos Impactos Socio-Econômicos da Automação Microelectrônica. São Paulo (mimeo), 1988; **A. Proença / H.M. Caulliraux,** Desintegração integrada: um novo padrão de organização? Rio de Janeiro: Universidade Federal, Instituto de Economia Industrial, 1989; **H. Schmitz / R. Carvalho,** Fordism is alive in Brazil, IDS Bulletin, Vol. 20, No. 4, 1989; **E.B. Silva,** Automation and Work Organization: Contrasts in Brazilian and British Car Factories, in: H. Schmitz / J. Cassiolato (eds.), Hi-Tech for Industrial Development. Lessons from the Brazilian Experience in Electronics and Automation. London, New York: Routledge, 1992; **J.R. Tauile,** Notes on Microelectronic Automation in Brazil, Cepal Review, No. 36, pp. 49-59, 1988; **idem,** Novos Padrões tecnológicos, competividade industrial e bem estar social: perspectivas brasileiras. Rio de Janeiro: Universidade Federal, Instituto da Economia Industrial, 1989.

7   **A. Fleury,** The impacts of microelectronics ... op. cit.; **J.R. Tauile,** Notes on Microelectronic ... op. cit.

8   **U. Jürgens et al.,** Moderne Zeiten in der Automobilfabrik. Strategien der Produktionsmodernisierung im Länder- und Konzernvergleich. Berlin, Heidelberg: Springer, 1989.

9   **H. Schmitz / R. Carvalho,** Fordism ... op. cit.

10 **R.R. Lima,** Implementing the "Just in Time" Production ... op. cit.; **A. Posthuma.** Japanese Production Techniques in Brazilian Automobile Components Firms: A Best

Practice Model or Basis for Adaptation? Paper Presented to the Conference on "Organisation and Control of the Labour Process" Aston University, March 28-30, 1990.

11   **A. Fleury / M. Salerno,** Condicionantes e Indutores ... op. cit.

12   **H. Schmitz / R. Carvalho,** Fordism ... op. cit.; **R.R. Lima,** Implementing the "Just in Time" Production ... op. cit.

13   **A. Fleury,** The impacts of microelectronics ... op. cit.; see also **A.G. Alves Filho et al.,** Fordism ..., op. cit.

14   See "O fantasma da obsolescência assusta o país", Exame, 13.12.1989.

15   **R. Semler,** Virando a própria mesa. São Paulo: Editora Best Seller, 1988; **idem,** Managing without Managers. Harvard Business Review, No. 5, pp. 76-84, 1989.

16   **A. Fleury / M. Salerno,** Condicionantes e Indutores ... op. cit.

17   **J. Humphrey,** New forms of work organization in industry: their implications for labour use and control in Brazil. Paper presented to conference on "Padrões Technológicas e Políticas de Gestâo", São Paulo, August 16-17, 1989.

18   **A. Fleury / M. Salerno,** Condicionantes e Indutores ... op. cit.

19   **BNDES,** Questóes Relativas à Competitividade da Indústria de Bens de Capital: Bens de Capital sob Encomenda e Máquinas-Ferramenta. Rio de Janeiro: BNDES / AP-DEEST, 1988.

20   Exame, Agosto 1990, p. 211.

21   **M. Porteous,** Revolution in a Recession? Advanced Technologies and Brazil's Machine Tool Sector in the Crises; **A. Fleury,** The impacts of microelectronics ... op. cit.

22   "Produção de maquinas cai 70 per cent; setor pede apoio ao Congresso", Folha de Sâo Paulo, 07.03.91.

23   Ibid.

24   **H.N. Cruz / M.E. Silva,** A Situação do Setor de Bens de Capital e suas Perspectivas, no place given, (mimeo), 1990.

25   **Cf. Costa / S. Mossri,** "Salario minimo . ", Folha de Sâo Paulo, 17.03.91.

26   "Voith demite e culpa inadimplencia estatal", Folha de Sâo Paulo, 07.03.91.

27   **H.N. Cruz / M.E. Silva,** A Situaçâo do Setor ... op. cit.

28   According to data in **P. Wogart,** LDCs move into human capital intensive industries. Kiel Working Papers, The Kiel Institute of World Economics, No. 393, 1989.

29   It is somewhat strange that two other MRP users explained that linking MRP with internal just-in-time is not feasible.

30   **C. Netz,** Muitas pedras e poco ouro nas empresas. Exame, 12 de Dezembro 1990.

31   It should be pointed out, however, that we obtained our findings mainly from interviews with management representatives. As **M. Leite** (O trabalhador e a máquina ... op. cit.) found out in a case study, management representatives may present innovations as their own achievements when they were actually the result of years of struggle by the workforce.

Technological Modernization Processes in Korean Small- and Medium-Scale Industry - a New Success Story?

Wolfgang Hillebrand

Studies describing Korea's rise in the past 25 years from being one of the poorest developing countries to the status of a young industrialized country focus almost entirely on the large conglomerates deliberately promoted by the state as the key actors in this process. The current debate in Korea is also characterized by concern about the continuing unchecked advance of the conglomerates and their growing economic and political power.

1   Trends since the Mid-70s

When actual trends are examined, however, a more complex picture emerges (Table 1):

- The large enterprises (with more than 300 employees) expanded primarily in the period from 1963-73. In 1973, for example, this group (of about 1,000 enterprises) accounted for some 60 per cent of the industrial labour force, 73 per cent of value added in industry and 63 per cent of exports.

- After 1973 the trend changed significantly. In just 17 years the number of small firms (5 to 19 employees) and medium-sized enterprises (20 to 299 employees) almost tripled from about 22,000 to 62,000 in 1990, when they accounted for about 58 per cent of the industrial labour force, 42.5 per cent of value added in industry and 45.5 per cent of exports - after a low of only 28 per cent in 1985.

The fact that the statistics also cover medium-sized enterprises belonging to the conglomerates does not in any way explain this trend. The change of trend in 1973, which has yet to be properly analysed, is likely to have been largely due to four sets of factors:

- favourable conditions for the development of the labour-intensive consumer goods industries, which have benefited from persistently high economic growth, a growing population, rising consumer incomes and a domestic market generally protected against foreign competition,

- large-scale industry's growing need for supplies due to the expansion of sectors manufacturing intermediate inputs, capital goods and electronics from the mid-70s,

- the substantial increase in government promotion from the late 1970s, which at least reduced the discrimination against small and medium-sized enterprises under the economic policy, and

- the growing ability, particularly of medium-sized enterprises, to penetrate foreign markets from the mid-80s.

Table 1 - Key Indicators of Korean Manufacturing Industries by Company Size[a], 1963 - 1990

	1963	1973	1980	1985	1988	1990[b]
Number of companies (1 000)						
- SMEs	18.1	22.3	29.8	43.0	60.4[c]	62.0
- LEs	0.2	1.0	1.0	1.1	1.4	...
Employees (1 000)						
- SMEs	267	457	1 000	1 368	1 847	...
- LEs	135	701	1 015	1 070	1 365	...
Employees (% of total)						
- SMEs	66.4	39.5	49.6	56.1	57.5	58.0
- LEs	33.6	60.5	50.4	43.9	42.5	42.0
Value added (% of total)						
- SMEs	51.6	27.2	35.2	37.6	42.6	42.5
- LEs	48.4	72.8	64.8	62.4	57.4	57.5
Exports (% of total)						
- SMEs	23.0[d]	37.3	32.1	27.8	36.0	45.5
- LEs	77.0[d]	62.7	67.9	72.2	64.0	54.5

[a] small business: 5 to 19 employees; medium business: 20 to 299 employees
[b] preliminary data
[c] estimated number of small businesses in 1988: 32 000
[d] figure for 1965

Source: Economic Planning Board, Industrial Bank of Korea

If the government has its way, the role played by small and medium-sized enterprises will continue to grow until the year 2000. By then they should be employing 72 per cent of the labour force and accounting for 58 per cent of value added in industry. This would be roughly the same as the situation in Japan in 1987.

2   Heavy Pressure to Modernize on a Weak Technological Base

Like Korean industry as a whole, small- and medium-scale industry has been undergoing a difficult restructuring process since the late 80s. The main problems to be overcome include

- the enormous rise in costs due to the persistently high rates of increase in unit labour costs since 1987, high capital market interest rates and rising land prices and rents,

- a growing shortage of labour due to the economy's tendency to over-heat and the fact that workers now prefer employment in large-scale industry or the service sector,

- growing competition from imports due to the - albeit cautious -opening of the domestic market,

- the fiercer competition in foreign markets both from other newly industrializing countries and new competitors (People's Republic of China, Indonesia, Thailand) and from the industrialized countries them-selves,

- low growth in the USA, still the most important market for Korean goods.

The strategy to be adopted if small- and medium-scale industry is to hold its own in the domestic and foreign markets in the future is clear: rapid restructuring of manufacturing to give better-quality products, combined with a sharp rise in productivity through the improvement of management methods, comprehensive modernization of the capital stock and the use of modern technologies. Implementing a strategy of this kind will, however, be too much for many traditional firms, and they face difficult times. The main winners in the process of structural change will be the still small group of medium-sized enterprises that have already attained or are about to attain international standards of efficiency.

Table 2 - Indicators of R & D Activity in Korean Manufacturing Industries by Company Size[a], 1988

Company Size / Indicators	- 99	100 - 299	300 - 999	1000 +	Total
1. R & D departments/ institutes (number)	412	503	348	231	1 494
2. R & D personell (number)	2 750	5 218	7 485	30 559	46 012
3. R & D personell (% of total R & D) personell in industry)	6.0	11.3	16.3	66.4	100
4. R & D expenditure (Mio. US $)[b]	77.5	157.5	278.2	1 654.0	2 167
5. Average R & D expenditure per company (1 000 US $)	188	312	797	7 191	
6. R & D expenditure (% of industry total	3.6	7.3	12.8	76.3	100
7. R & D expenditure (% of total sales)	5.08	2.01	1.47	1.89	1.88[c]

[a] Data include only the companies which responded to a survey of the Ministry of Science and Technology conducted in 1989. The survey focused on companies with more than 100 employees, but also included companies with less than 100 employees but with systematic R & D activity.
[b] Calculated on the basis of 680 Won per US $.
[c] Industry average.

Source: Based on the Report on the Survey of Research and Development in Science and Technology, Seoul 1990, pp. 161 and 201

Even those who know Korean industry well hesitate to say how large this group is. However, it is unlikely to comprise more than 3,000 to 5,000 enterprises, most of which produce parts, with only a few manufacturing end products.

The assumption that the number of highly competitive small and medium-sized enterprises is still very small is also confirmed by analyses of R&D potential in Korean industry. Estimates by the Ministry of Trade and Industry indicate that only about 10 per cent of Korean SMEs, or some 6,000 enterprises, undertook research and development activities in 1987. The number of enterprises continuously and systematically engaging in R&D is far smaller. A survey carried out by the Ministry of Science and

Technology showed that only about 900 small and medium-sized enterprises had an R&D department in 1989. This group (see Table 2) accounted for only

- 16 per cent of R&D personnel in manufacturing industry and

- 11 per cent of manufacturing industry's expenditure on R&D.

What should not be overlooked in any interpretation of these figures, however, is that until the early 80s there was little or no R&D in Korean manufacturing industry. Even total expenditure on R&D by the four largest conglomerates (Hyundai, Samsung, Lucky Goldstar, Daewoo) barely exceeded US$ 100 million in 1980. The 80s can thus be regarded as the decade in which at least a few small and medium-sized enterprises first began to take an interest in R&D.

3   Reaction Potential and External Competitive Threats in the Footwear, Machine Tool and Personal Computer Industries

The fact that Korea's manufacturing industry consists of a very heterogeneous range of enterprises was also revealed by a study carried out in early 1991 by a working group from the German Development Institute in which technological modernization processes in the sports shoe, machine tool and PC industries were analysed.[1]

It was found that all three sectors were dominated by a small number of highly competitive fairly large to large enterprises. In 1990

- the five largest enterprises in the export-oriented sports shoe industry accounted for about a third of output and some 45 per cent of exports,

- eight to ten fairly large enterprises accounted for two thirds of output in the inward-oriented machine tool industry and

- six fairly large enterprises accounted for about 90 per cent of output and exports in the export-oriented PC industry.

It was also found that the number of highly competitive small and medium-sized enterprises (manufacturing end products) is still very small, hardly more than 20 in each of the three sectors according to Korean sectoral

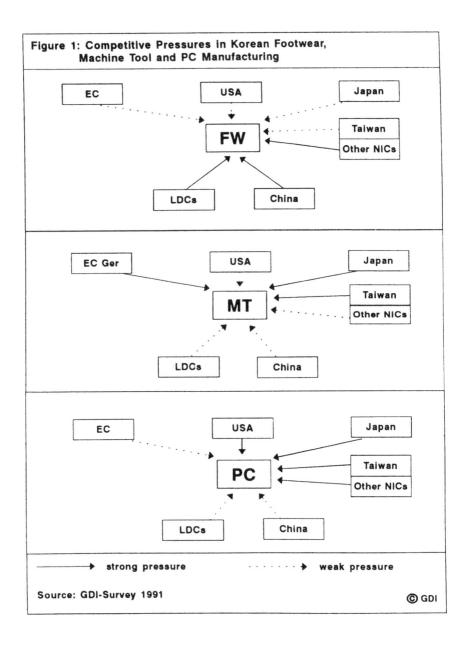

Figure 1: Competitive Pressures in Korean Footwear, Machine Tool and PC Manufacturing

specialists (see also Tables 1 and 2 in the annex). Like the dominant large enterprises, these medium-sized "promising enterprises" have a good chance of coping with competitive pressures from abroad. This pressure is due (see the diagram),

- in the sports shoe industry, to newly industrializing countries (particularly Thailand), less developed countries (particularly Indonesia) and the People's Republic of China,

- in the machine tool industry, to Japan, Germany and Taiwan and

- in the PC industry, to Japan, the USA and such NICs as Taiwan, Singapore and Hong Kong.

The chances of the many traditional and marginal enterprises (about 850 sports shoe, 840 machine tool and 200 to 600 PC manufacturers) withstanding the growing pressure of competition must, on the other hand, be viewed with scepticism.

4   Competitive Strategies of Modern Medium-sized Footwear, Machine Tool and Personal Computer Manufacturers

Korean small and medium-sized enterprises wanting to hold their ground in the constantly growing competition in the domestic and foreign markets will not be able to rely on low labour costs as a major parameter of competition in the future. However, becoming more competitive calls for more than just technological innovations. As the debate on "flexible specialization" that has been going on in the western industrialized countries for years and the more recent debate on "lean production" have shown, there is a greater need for a broadly based competitive strategy that seeks to combine "best practice technology" and "best practice organization of production".[2] Whether enterprises are large, medium-sized or small, the most important determinants of success appear to include

- systematic corporate planning based on an analysis of the specific strengths and weaknesses of the enterprise,

- clear market and customer orientation,

- a management concept emphasizing the continuing training of the workforce, and lean organizational structures,

- close interaction between research, development, manufacturing and marketing to ensure short lead times, low-cost production and success in the market,

- continuous product and process innovations,

- exploitation of the potential of new technologies (flexible automation, such CA technologies as CAD, CAM and CAQ, office automation),

- a consciously structured division of labour among enterprises, based on a careful definition of the relationship between what an enterprise can do itself and what it should buy in from outside, given its strengths and weaknesses,

- optimal synchronization of production and input supply to reduce storage and financing costs and

- the integration of enterprises into a conducive environment.[3]

With this frame of reference in the background, the analysis of the medium-term competitive strategies of 36 enterprises (13 footwear, 13 machine tool and 10 PC manufacturers), 30 of which are modern small and medium-sized firms, revealed the following (see Table 3):

1) Overall competitive position: 20 of the 36 enterprises regarded them-selves as leaders in their sector, the other 16 as a good average. Asked about their international competitiveness, nine footwear manufacturers felt they achieved international efficiency standards, as against only two machine tool and three personal computer manufacturers.

2) Overall corporate strategy: with a few exceptions (about five to seven enterprises), it was found that the enterprises interviewed had begun to implement relatively comprehensive medium-term (1991-1993) moderniza-tion strategies to improve their competitiveness. It must be emphasized, however, that the survey focused on an analysis of measures that enterprises were planning to take by 1993 to improve their competitiveness. How capable they are of actually implementing their ambitious plans remains to be seen. Nonetheless, it can be said that the general tendency of the planned measures shows them to be commensurate with the frame of reference of the "flexible specialization" strategy.

3) Reform of corporate management: the Korean management style has traditionally featured autocratic leadership, top-down decision-making and

Table 3 – Main Features of the Technological Modernization Strategies of the Companies Surveyed

	Footwear Manuf.		Machine Tool Manuf.		PC Manufact.	
	1990	91/93	1990	91/93	1990	91/93
I. Intra-Firm Reorganization						
1. New management concepts	(x)	x	x	xx	xx	xxx
2. Market / product strategy						
o lower end of market	-	-	x	x	xx	x
o middle of the market	xx	x	xxx	xxx	xxx	xx
o higher end of market	xx	xxx	x(x)	xx	-	xx
3. Market orientation						
o domestic market	(x)	x	xxx	xxx	x	xx
o exports	xxx	xxx	(x)	x	xxx	xxx
4. Manpower training						
o in-house	xxx	xxx	xxx	xxx	xxx	xxx
o training centers	x	x	xx	xx	xxx	xxx
o R & D institutes	x	x	xx	xx(x)	xx	xx
5. R & D activities						
o in-house R & D	xxx	xxx	xxx	xxx	xxx	xxx
o links to local centres	x(x)	x(x)	xx	xx	xx	xx
o links to local companies	xx	xx	x(x)	x(x)	x	x
o links to overseas centres	xx	xx	x(x)	x(x)	xx	xx
o links to foreign companies	x(x)	x(x)	x(x)	xx	xx	xx
6. Factory automation / OA						
o use of CAD	(x)	x(x)	x(x)	xx	x	xx
o use of CAM	-	(x)	(x)	x(x)	x	x
o FMS	-	-	-	x	-	(x)
o office automation	x(x)	xx	x	xx	xxx	xxx
7. Internal logistics	-	x	x	x	x(x)	x(x)
II. Inter-Firm Linkages						
1. R & D cooperation with local companies	x(x)	xx	x(x)	xx	x	x
2. R & D cooperation with foreign companies	x(x)	x(x)	x(x)	xx	xx	xx
3. Use of just-in time	-	(x)	-	(x)	-	(x)
III. Conduciveness of the National Business Environment						
1. Public support structures	xx	xx	xx	xx	x(x)	xx
2. Domestic R & D base	x(x)	xx	xx	xx	xx	xx

Key: - not relevant; x not so important; xx important; xxx very important

Source: Assessments of GDI research team

strict supervision of the workforce. The need for a change to a new management style or a new corporate identity is recognized by the majority of enterprises; practical implementation differed in the various sectors.

Reform of the management style and organizational structures was farthest advanced among the PC manufacturers. More decentralized decision-making structures, group work, the delegation of more responsibility to shop floor level and generally leaner organizational structures had already been introduced at the time of the survey or were to be introduced by 1993. In the machine tool sector the situation was similar, although the implementation of the reform of corporate management was still in its very early stages. Compared with the two engineering industries, awareness of the need for reforms in the areas of management and organization was far less developed among the footwear manufacturers. Only a few of them, i.e. four or five enterprises, were planning such reforms.

4) Market and customer orientation: the need for comprehensive market and customer orientation was recognized by almost all the enterprises:

-      The footwear manufacturers intend to concentrate on the top end of the market and to remain highly export-oriented. They will therefore be stepping up their efforts to defend their threatened position in the USA, their most important foreign market, and to improve their position in Japan, the European Community and Eastern Europe.

       For machine tool manufacturers the middle market segment remains crucial, since their technological base is still too weak for them to be able to manufacture top-qua-lity products (requiring a high level of precision and durability). Nonetheless, almost all the enterprises inter-viewed are preparing to change to the manufacture of high-quality standard CNC machines. With the domestic market booming, the pressure to penetrate foreign markets is low. Despite this, ten of the thirteen manufacturers are planning to sell to East and South-East Asian markets in the future. The USA (seven manufacturers) and Japan and the European Community (five manufacturers each) are also to figure more prominently in future sales planning.

       As product cycles in the personal computer sector are very short, PC manufacturers will survive only if they succeed in rising to the upper market segment fairly quickly. Plummeting prices in the world PC market and the resulting cut-throat competition will, however, make it difficult for them to continue gearing production almost entirely to export markets. All the enterprises interviewed are therefore trying to gain a firm foothold in the rapidly expanding domestic market, concentrating on the middle market segment, where the demand is.

On the whole, it was apparent that the enterprises interviewed in all three sectors had developed clear ideas on their product and market strategies until 1993. The same can be said of other important aspects seen today as forming part of promising marketing concepts. Thus all the enterprises intend to become more competitive in the future in terms of both prices and technology, to develop cooperative relationships with their customers, to improve their corporate image and to step up sales under their own brand names.

5) Personnel development and R&D orientation: the most important assets that competing enterprises have are the skills and motivation of their workforce. Both must be constantly developed or activated. By far the most important means of developing personnel referred to by the enterprises interviewed was internal training. Additional training measures at local centres and R&D institutions were important primarily for the PC and machine tool manufacturers. To improve the motivation and skills of their workforce, the majority of the enterprises intend to introduce more flexible working practices, such as job rotation and/or job enrichment or enlargement, to a greater degree in the future.

As well as taking such personnel development measures, almost all enterprises have stepped up their R&D activities in recent years. Of the 36 enterprises, 34 had already established R&D departments of their own. As a proportion of total turnover, spending on R&D, still very low in the late 80s, particularly among the footwear and machine tool manufacturers, is to be significantly increased by 1993. The plans indicate that it will reach at least 3 per cent in most cases, with the PC manufacturers even intending to raise it to around 10 per cent.

6) R&D management: higher spending on R&D does not in any way guarantee the efficient use of R&D resources. This depends on the quality of R&D management. Given their limited resources, the main problem for small and medium-sized enterprises is to strike the right balance between in-house R&D and the use of external R&D services. The findings of the study indicate that most of the enterprises have good prospects of coping with this difficult balancing act, principally because they have begun to make selective use of external R&D services on the basis of their own clear R&D commitment.

- Among the footwear manufacturers cooperation with both local R&D institutions and domestic enterprises was already fairly well advanced. In addition, eight of the thirteen enterprises were already cooperating with R&D institutions or enterprises abroad. Seven intended to cooperate more closely with foreign enterprises, particularly in Japan.

- The interviews with the machine tool manufacturers revealed a similar situation. Nine of the thirteen enterprises had concrete plans for closer cooperation, particularly with Japanese and German enterprises.

- Although the PC manufacturers were using local R&D centres, they saw foreign enterprises and R&D centres as their most important external sources of technology. Seven of the ten PC manufacturers were planning to cooperate more closely with US and Japanese manufacturers. Cooperation with European firms attracted little interest.

A second strategically important problem whose solution also depends on the quality of R&D management is the "correct" distribution of R&D resources among the areas of product innovation and development and process innovation and development. The responses from the enterprises on this aspect of R&D management suggest that they will be placing equal emphasis on product and process innovations.

7) **Factory and office automation:** like the western industrialized countries, Korea intends to take every advantage of the potential of flexible manufacturing technologies to increase efficiency. Since the mid-90s "factory automation (FA)" and "office automation (OA)" have been among the dominant subjects in the debate on industrial policy.

The high hopes pinned on the introduction of computer-assisted methods in the manufacturing and administrative sectors of enterprises were also revealed by the survey. Nearly all the enterprises are hoping for a significant improvement in their general competitive position, and especially for an increase in productivity, greater flexibility and speed of reaction and an improvement in the quality of their products. However, they are also aware of many serious obstacles, particularly to the rapid introduction of FA, the main ones being inadequately trained personnel, the lack of adequate software at reasonable costs and - a problem especially faced by machine tool manufacturers - the high cost of hardware (e.g. flexible manufacturing systems). Consequently, the use of flexible manufacturing technologies was far from widespread in 1990:

- The level of automation in 12 enterprises (seven footwear and five PC manufacturers) was very low (1st automation level/low-cost automation). Only a few, very simple automatic machines without electronic controls were being used.

- Nineteen enterprises, including 12 of the 13 machine tool manufacturers, were using advanced, but not yet interlinked machine tools with NC or CNC controls (2nd automation level).

- Only two enterprises (one large machine tool manufacturer and one large PC manufacturer) had already automated at least one production line and begun to introduce CAM (3rd automation level). A more comprehensive concept of factory automation (4th automation level) did not exist in any of the enterprises interviewed.

- The main CA technologies used were CAD systems (eight machine tool and seven PC manufacturers, but only two footwear manufacturers). The introduction of CAM had begun in only two enterprises (see above).

The plans of the enterprises reveal that significant changes are unlikely before 1993. Only three of the fairly large machine tool manufacturers and one large PC manufacturer intend to automate their production processes fully by 1993 and to combine this with modern concepts of internal and inter-company logistics and advanced methods of office automation (4th automation level). Where CA technologies are concerned, the number of CAD and CAM systems in particular will rise. By 1993 CAD is to be introduced by 26 enterprises, i.e. all the machine tool manufacturers, eight PC manufacturers and five footwear manufacturers. The number of CAM systems is to rise from 2 to 15 (6 PC, 5 machine tool and 4 footwear manufacturers). Compared with factory automation, office automation, having already been introduced on some considerable scale by 1990, continues its rapid advance. Thus almost all the PC and machine tool manufacturers and seven footwear manufacturers intend to introduce fairly comprehensive computer-assisted methods to rationalize clerical and administrative activities by 1993.

The generally very cautious attitude towards the introduction of flexible manufacturing technologies is not altogether surprising, since they are very new to Korean enterprises. As in the industrialized countries, the potential of flexible automation can be effectively tapped only after long and painful learning processes. What seems important, however, is that most of the small and medium-sized modern enterprises interviewed are obviously prepared to undertake this arduous task.

8) Organization of the inter-company division of labour: in the western industrialized countries the inter-company division of labour is increasingly based on sophisticated inter-company logistics. Large enterprises in particular have a growing image of themselves as "system integrators" who concentrate on a few core functions (R&D, systems development, the manufacture of complex and technologically demanding components), while integrating a large number of suppliers into a tight production and innovation network. Although there are already numerous examples of larger medium-sized manufacturers also evolving into "system integrators", it must be said, by and large, that small and medium-sized enterprises in the OECD countries are taking nothing like full advantage of the rationalization potential of such concepts as just-in-time. It therefore came as no surprise to find that just-in-time concepts are not yet in widespread use in the Korean enterprises interviewed. Only four (three fairly large PC manufacturers and one large machine tool manufacturer) stated that their relations with suppliers were already organized on just-in-time lines (1990). However, another eight enterprises intended to introduce just-in-time by 1993. The conclusion to be drawn is that the medium-sized modern enterprises interviewed are in the process of establishing a fairly tight inter-company innovation network (see point 6) rather than a tight production network.

9) Korea's quality as an industrial location: the manufacturing efficiency of an enterprise depends on far more than the thorough rationalization of the production process and a consciously structured inter-company division of labour. The quality of the industrial location is equally crucial. Where the macro level is concerned, Korea's quality in this respect has fallen sharply in recent years (see Chapter 2). Even so, as is evident from the machine tool industry, the enterprises can at least rely on a relatively dense network of private and public institutions to overcome critical constraints in R&D, personnel development, management, technology transfer, the procurement of information, marketing and financing (see Table 4). The footwear and PC manufacturers are able to use similar networks of supportive institutions. It therefore seems no exaggeration to say that competitiveness at micro level in the three sectors is improved by a well structured meso sector. It remains

Table 4 – Importance of Private and Public Support Structures (Machine Tool Manufacturing)

Support areas	Business Associations		Public Bodies						Institutions for SME Support	
	KOMMA	KOAMI	KIMM	KAIST	KIST	KPC	KIET	KOTRA	SMIPC	IBK
1. R&D			xxx	xx					x	
2. Training			x		x	xxx			xx	
3. Management						xxx			xxx	
4. Technology transfer	x		xx		x				xx	
5. Information gathering								xx		
6. Marketing (domestic)	xxx	xx					xxx			
7. Marketing (international)	xx	x					xxx			
8. Finance							xx	xxx	x	
9. Lobbying	xxx	xx	x						xx	xxx

KOMMA: Korea Machine Tool Manufacturers' Association
KOAMI: Korea Association of Machinery Industry
KIMM: Korea Institute of Machinery and Metals
KAIST: Korea Advanced Institute of Science and Technology
KIST: Korea Institute of Science and Technology
KPC: Korea Productivity Centre
KIET: Korea Institute for Economics and Technology
KOTRA: Korea Trade Organization
SMIPC: Small and Medium Industry Promotion Corporation
IBK: Industrial Bank of Korea

Key: x some support; xx important support; xxx very important support

Source: Assessments of experts close to the machine tool industry

to be seen, however, whether this will be enough for international standards of efficiency to be attained, given the deterioration in the general business environment (high rates of wage increase, high inflation, high financing costs and rents, a shortage of highly skilled workers).

10) Conclusions: the competitive strategies of the 36 enterprises interviewed are highly commensurate with the frame of reference of the "flexible specialization" strategy, although little notice has so far been taken in Korea of the debate on new production concepts. The competitive strength of the enterprises studied is based primarily on

- a fairly clearly formulated medium-term corporate strategy,

- purposeful market and customer orientation,

- comprehensive rationalization of the production process and of clerical and administrative functions, combined with a clear commitment in the areas of personnel development and R&D, and

- good R&D management, which skilfully combines internal and external potential, for example.

On the other hand, the use of modern technologies, especially flexible automation techniques, is still in its infancy. Far more advanced is the application of computer-assisted technologies in office automation. The rationalization potential of a consciously structured inter-company division of labour is being tapped principally in the area of R&D. As is true of the majority of medium-sized enterprises in the OECD countries, such modern logistical concepts as just-in-time are hardly used at present.

Competitiveness at micro level continues to be supported by a well structured meso sector. Serious threats to competitiveness are emerging from the now far less favourable general environment (macro level). The only medium-sized enterprises likely to cope with these threats will be those which are capable of formulating and implementing highly complex competitive strategies. In all likelihood many traditional and marginal enterprises will be unable to withstand the growing pressure of competition. It is therefore to be feared that Korean small- and medium-scale industry will come under considerable pressure to adjust in the 90s and that the success story of the past fifteen years will not continue.

Notes

1   See **W. Hillebrand et al.**, Technological Modernization in Small and Medium Industries in Korea with Special Emphasis on the Role of International Enterprise Cooperation,
Berlin 1992.

2   For the effects of the new concepts of production and organization on the competitive
position of newly industrializing countries see **W. Hillebrand,** Industrielle und technologische   Anschlußstrategien   in   teilindustrialisierten   Ländern.   Bewertung   der
allokationstheoretischen Kontroverse und Schlussfolgerungen aus der Fallstudie Republik
Korea, Berlin 1991. For the concept of flexible specialization see, in particular, **H.
Schmitz,** Flexible Specialization - A New Paradigm of Small-Scale Industrialization?,
Institute of Development Studies, Discussion Paper 261, Sussex 1989, and for the
concept of lean production **J.P. Womack / D.T. Jones / D. Roos,** The Machine that
Changed the World, New York 1990.

3   For the determinants of international competitiveness see **W. Hillebrand,** op. cit., Part
I, and the contribution of **D. Messner** in this paper.

Annex Tables

Table 1 – The Korean Footwear, Machine Tool and PC Industry Selected Indicators, 1988 – 1990			
Year	1988	1989	1990[a]
Footwear Industry			
Production (million US $)	4 200	4 000	4 800
Exports (million US $)	3 800	3 600	4 300
Imports (million US $)	55	75[a]	110
Employment (1 000)	158	...	...
Machine Tool Industry			
Production (million US $)	632	760	1 000
Exports (million US $)	57	116	70
Imports (million US $)	609	760	...
Employment (1 000)	21[a]	25[a]	30[a]
PC Industry			
Production (million US $)	1 087	1 196	960
Local sales (million US $)	150	220[a]	350
Exports (million US $)	937	976	610
Imports (million US $)	70	...	...
Local sales (units/1 000)	180	250	520
Exports (units/1 000)	1 900	2 000	1 300
Employment (1 000)	8 - 10[a]	...	...
[a] estimates			
Sources: KOAMI, EIAK, various economic journals			

Table 2 - Enterprise Structure in Footwear, Machine Tool (MT) and
         PC Manufacturing

Company Groups	Approximate number of companies (1990)			
	Sports shoes	Leather shoes	MT	PC
Top performers/ dominant producers	5 LEs	11 LEs	8 - 10 LEs	6 LEs
Promising enterprises	<u>40</u> - 15 LEs - 25 SMEs	<u>25</u> - 5 LEs - 20 SMEs	<u>20</u> - 20 SMEs	<u>20 - 25</u> - 4 LEs - 20 SMEs
Traditional producers	500	250	30 - 40	-
Marginal producers	350	200	800	320 - 600
Approximate total number	900	500	850	230 - 600

Source: GDI Survey 1991; industry specialists; secondary data

GDI-Publications of Related Interest

Occasional Papers (1987 - 1992)

Kampffmeyer, T., Towards a Solution of the Debt Crisis. Applying the Concept of Corporate Composition with Creditors, No. 89, Berlin 1987, 151 p. (ISBN 3-88985-047-2) E/G*

Ashoff, G., Industrial Development and Industrial Policies of Small Development Countries - the Case of the Dominican Republic, No. 92, Berlin 1988, 197 p. (ISBN 3-88985-051-0) E/G

Kürzinger, E., Argentina. Blocked Development, No. 94, Berlin 1988, 68 p. (ISBN 3-88985-058-8) E/G

Esser, K., Welt- und Regionalmarktorientierung - Empfehlungen zur regionalen Kooperation und Integration, No. 98, Berlin 1990, 83 p. (ISBN 3-88985-062-6) G

of interest:

-, Hacia la competitividad industrial en América Latina: el aspecto de cooperación y integración regional, in: INTAL/BID, integración latinoamericana, Vol. 14, No. 48, Buenos Aires, Aug. 1989, pp. 16 - 41 S

-, Desafíos de una inserción activa en la economía mundial para los países de América Latina, Fundación Friedrich Ebert, Renglones de Gestión de Desarrollo, No. 5, Lima, Sept. 1989, 45 p. S

-, Perspectivas económicas para América Latina en la próxima década, Österreichisches Lateinamerika-Institut/OLAI, Wien, Instituto de Relaciones Europeo-Latinoamericanas/IRELA, Madrid, Consejo Europeo de Investigaciones Sociales sobre América Latina/CEISAL, Baden, Oct. 29th - 30th, 1990, 9 p. S

-, "Integración flexible" o "integración regional", Papel para la XXIX Reunión del Consejo Asesor del Presidente del BID para Asuntos de Integración, Mendoza, Jan. 6th - 8th, 1991, 8 p. S

-, Why Integration Matters: "Market Mechanism plus X" and "Free Trade Area plus X", Inter-American Development Bank, XXX Meeting of The President's Advisory Committee on Integration Matters, Washington, D.C., Berlin, July 16th, 1992, 6 p. E

Messner, D. / L. Mármora, La integración de Argentina, Brasil y Uruguay: concepciones, objectivos, resultados, in: Comercio Exterior, Vol. 41, No. 2, Mexiko, Febr. 1991, p. 155 - 166; Nueva Sociedad, No. 113, Caracas 1991, pp. 130 - 145 S

Hillebrand, W., Industrielle und technologische Anschlußstrategien in teilindustrialisierten Ländern. Bewertung der allokationstheoretischen Kontroverse und Schlußfolgerungen aus der Fallstudie Republik Korea, No. 100, Berlin 1991, 226 p. (ISBN 3-88985-066-9) G

of interest:

-, The Newly Industrializing Economies as Models for Establishing a Highly Competitive Industrial Base - What Lessons to Learn?, in: M. Kulessa (Ed.), The Newly Industrializing Economies of Asia - Prospects of Co-operation, Springer-Verlag, Berlin et al., 1990, pp. 249 - 262 E

-, Por qué se industrializaron? Lecciones de Corea y Taiwán para América Latina? in: Development and Cooperation, No. 2, Bonn 1990, pp. 15 - 16 E

Messner, D. / L. Mármora, Old Development Theories - New Concepts of Internationalization. A Comparison between Argentina and South Korea, in: W. Väth (Ed.), Political Regulation in the "Great Crisis", Berlin 1989, pp. 131 - 173 E/G

-, Los escombros teóricos de la investigación del desarrollo - Una comparación entre Argentina y Corea del Sur, in: Nueva Sociedad, No. 110, Caracas 1990, pp. 15 - 23 S

Working Papers (1989 - 1992)

Ashoff, G., Die Entwicklungszusammenarbeit zwischen der Europäischen Gemeinschaft und Lateinamerika. Erfahrungen und Perspektiven, Berlin 1988, 159 p. G

of interest:

-, La cooperación para el desarrollo entre la Comunidad Europea y América Latina: Experiencias y perspectivas, in: GDI/Instituto de Relaciones Europeo-Latinoamericanas/IRELA, Documento de Trabajo No. 16, Madrid 1989, pp. 120 - 138; also in: Revista de Estudios Europeos, No. 11, Ciudad de ha Habana 1989, 181 p. S

-, Ni especiales, ni privilegiadas sino mejores relaciones - Cooperación para el Desarrollo CE-A.L., in: Nueva Sociedad, No. 106, Caracas, March-April 1990, pp. 172 - 182 S

Esser, K. (Ed.), Argentinien. Zum industriepolitischen Suchprozeß seit 1983, Berlin, March 1989, 168 p. G

Esser, K., Perú. Una salida de la crisis, Berlin, June 1989, 40 p. S/G

of interest:

-, Perú: Una salida de la crisis, Fundación Friedrich Ebert, Renglones de Gestión de Desarrollo, No. 9, Lima, Sept. 1989, 85 p. S

-, Economía Social de Mercado: Una salida de la crisis para el Perú?, in: R. Abusada S., et al., Retos de política económica frente a la crisis social. Perspectivas para los Años 90, Habitat Perú Siglo XXI/Fundación Friedrich Naumann, Lima 1989, pp. 195 - 212 S

Caller Salas, J., Política económica y desarrollo productivo. Un análisis retrospectivo, INP/GTZ, Lima, May 1990, 94 p. S

Esser, K., Bundesrepublik Deutschland - Chile: entwicklungspolitische Zusammenarbeit, Berlin, Jan. 1990, 81 p. G

Meyer-Stamer, J., From Import Substitution to International Competitiveness - Brazil's Informatics Industry at the Crossroads, Berlin, March 1990, 103 p. E/G

of interest:

-, Unconventional Technology Transfer and High-Tech Development: The Case of Informatics in Newly-Industrializing Countries, in: M. Chatterji (Ed.), Technology Transfer in the Developing Countries, MacMillan, London 1990, pp. 281 - 290 E

-, Kompetenter Staat, wettbewerbsfähige Unternehmen: Die Schaffung dynamischer komparativer Vorteile in der ostasiatischen Elektronikindustrie, in: Nord-Süd aktuell, No. 4, Hamburg 1991, pp. 567 - 577 G

-, HDTV: Europas letzte Bastion gegen Japans Dominanz?, Vierteljahresberichte, No. 126, Bonn 1991, pp. 355 - 365 G

-, The end of Brazil's Informatics Policy, in: Science and Public Policy, Vol. 19, No. 2, April 1992, pp. 99 - 110 E

Messner, D., Uruguay: El sector industrial ante la apertura externa, Berlin, March 1990, 190 p. S/G

Ashoff, G., et al., Reconversión industrial y liberalización económica en Venezuela: un estudio de ramas industriales seleccionadas, Berlin 1991, 225 p. S/G

Kürzinger, E., et al., Política ambiental en México: el papel de las organizaciones no gubernamentales, Mexico 1991, 157 p. (ISBN 3-88-985-067-7) S/G

Meyer-Stamer, J. / C. Rauh / H. Riad / S. Schmitt / T. Welte, Comprehensive Modernization on the Shop Floor: A Case Study on the Brazilian Machinery Industry, Berlin 1991, 116 p. E/G

Esser, K., Development of a Competitive Strategy: A Challenge to the Countries of Latin America in the 1990s, Berlin, Sept. 1991, 41 p. E/S/G

of interest:

-, La inserción de América Latina en la economía mundial: integración "pasiva" o "activa"?, in: INTAL/BID, integración latinoamericana, Vol. 12, No. 126, Buenos Aires, Aug. 1987, pp. 17 - 46 S

-, La inserción de América Latina en la economía mundial, in: G. Martner (Ed.), América Latina en el mundo de mañana. Ambito international y regional, Editorial Nueva Sociedad, UNITAR/PROFAL, Caracas 1987, pp. 17 - 46 S

-, ¿Cómo dinamizar las relaciones económicas de América Latina? in: Instituto para la Integración de América Latina/INTAL, Comisión Económica para América Latina y el Caribe/CEPAL, América Latina en la economía mundial, Seminario en homenaje al Dr. Raúl Prebisch, CEPAL, Santiago de Chile 1988, pp. 229 - 246 S

-, Latin America in Crisis. Neo-Structuralism as an Economic Policy Response, in: Economics. A Biannual Collection of Recent German Contributions to the Field of Economic Science, Vol. 41, Tübingen 1990, pp. 39 - 61 E/S/G

-, "Institutional Responsiveness Seems Central to Success", Grupo de Trabajo de la Presidencia del BID sobre la Industrialización Latinoamericana, Nuevos Lineamentos de la Industrialización Latinoamericana en su Relación con el Banco Interamericano de Desarrollo, Washington, D.C., March 17th - 18th, 1991, 23 p. S

-, Latin America: Some Comments on Economic and Political Transition, in: Economics, Vol. 43, pp. 107 - 127 E/G

Messner, D. / Meyer-Stamer, J., Recipe for Success: Strong State and Strong Enterprises, in: Development and Cooperation, No. 2, Berlin 1992, pp. 14 - 16 E

Messner, D. / L. Mármora, Lessons from a Disaster? A Critique of Unidimensional Development Concepts, in: Economics, Vol. 45, Tübingen 1992, pp. 49 - 74 E

Messner, D., Hacia la competividad industrial en Chile - El caso de la industria de la madera, Berlin 1992, 204 p. S/G

of interest:

Messner, D., Chile en el camino difícil hacia la competitividad internacional - El desarrollo de la industria maderera, Discussion Paper, Berlin 1991, 24 p. S

-, Wirtschaftspolitsche Neuorientierung in Chile - Vom autoritären Neoliberalismus zu einer Strategie aktiver Weltmarktintegration, in: Journal für Entwicklungspolitik, No. 3, Wien 1992, pp. 135 - 148 **G**

Hillebrand, W., et al., Technological Modernization in Small and Medium Industries in Korea With Special Emphasis on the Role of International Enterprise Cooperation, GDI, Berlin 1992, 94 p. **E**

* E = English
 S = Spanish
 G = German

GDI-Books available in English

Radke, Detlef: Conditionality and Policy Dialogue in Development Cooperation, 91 p., Berlin 1985, ISBN 3-88985-041-3

Wiemann, Jürgen: India in Transition. Industrialization, Industrial Policy and Economic Cooperation (published by Allied Publishers Pvt. Ltd., New Delhi)

Ashoff, Guido / K. Esser: Argentina. Economic Cooperation with the Federal Republic of Germany and the European Community. Problems and Prospects, 153 p., Berlin 1985, ISBN 3 -88985-039-1

German Development Institute: Structural Distortions and Adjustment Programmes in the Poor Countries of Africa. A Challenge for Development Policy, 377 p., Berlin 1985, ISBN 3-88985-042-1

Wolff, Peter: Stabilization Policy and Structural Adjustment in Turkey, 1980 - 1985. The Role of IMF and World Bank in an Externally Supported Adjustment Process, 203 p., Berlin 1987, ISBN 3-88985-046-4

Zehender, Wolfgang: Regional Cooperation through Trade and Industry? The Prospects for Regional Economic Communities in West and Central Africa, 95 p., Berlin 1987, ISBN 3-88985-045-6

Kampffmeyer, Thomas: Towards a Solution of the Debt Crisis. Applying the Concept of Corporate Compositions with Creditors, 151 p., Berlin 1987, ISBN 3-88985-049-9

Schneider-Barthold, Wolfgang: Talking, Acting and Learning with the Poor. Grassroots Development in the Third World and its Promotion, 78 p., Berlin 1987, ISBN 3-88985-055-3

Wiemann, Jürgen: India. Self-imposed Restraint of Development Potential. 107 p., Berlin 1988, ISBN 3-88985-056-1

Kürzinger, Edith: Argentina. Blocked Development. 113 p., Berlin 1988. ISBN 3-88985-058-8

Hofmann, Michael: Saudi Arabia. Purchased Industrialization. 27 p., Berlin 1988, ISBN 3-88985-057-X

Claus, Burghard, et al.: Coordination of the Developmnt Cooperation Policies of Major OECD Donor Countries. 100 p., Berlin 1989, ISBN 3-88985-061-8

Wiemann, Jürgen: The Implications of the Uruguay Round and the Single Market for the European Community's Trade Policy towards Developing Countries. 45 p., Berlin 1990, ISBN 3-88985-063-4

Otzen, Uwe: Stabilization of Agricultural Resources. Concept, Requirements and Measures to Ensure Sustainable Agricultural Development, with Examples from Southern Africa, 143 p., Berlin 1992. ISBN 3-88985-070-7

For Product Safety Concerns and Information please contact our EU
representative GPSR@taylorandfrancis.com
Taylor & Francis Verlag GmbH, Kaufingerstraße 24, 80331 München, Germany

www.ingramcontent.com/pod-product-compliance
Ingram Content Group UK Ltd.
Pitfield, Milton Keynes, MK11 3LW, UK
UKHW042201240425
457818UK00011B/334